PENGUIN BOOKS

THE RELUCTANT FAMILY MAN

Nilima Chitgopekar is an associate professor in the department of history at Jesus and Mary College, Delhi University. She has authored six books and several articles and essays on Hindu gods and other related matters. She has been the recipient of prestigious fellowships from the Oxford Centre for Hindu Studies, the Charles Wallace India Trust and USIS, and has lectured widely in India and abroad. Chitgopekar has also worked with the BBC and been featured in their documentaries and radio programmes. More recently, in her attempt to take Hindu mythology to a far larger audience, she has been involved in making several online films of her lectures, which have been sold worldwide.

T0294321

Nilima Chitgopekar

THE
RELUCTANT
FAMILY MAN

SHIVA IN EVERYDAY LIFE

PENGUIN BOOKS

An imprint of Penguin Random House

PENGUIN BOOKS

USA | Canada | UK | Ireland | Australia
New Zealand | India | South Africa | China | Singapore

Penguin Books is part of the Penguin Random House group of companies
whose addresses can be found at global.penguinrandomhouse.com

Published by Penguin Random House India Pvt. Ltd
4th Floor, Capital Tower 1, MG Road,
Gurugram 122 002, Haryana, India

First published in Penguin Books by Penguin Random House India 2019

Copyright © Nilima Chitgopekar 2019
Illustrations copyright © Priyankar Gupta 2019

While every effort has been made to verify the authenticity of the information
contained in this book, the publisher and the author are in no way liable for
the use of the information contained herein.

ISBN 9780143443216

Typeset in Adobe Garamond Pro by Manipal Digital Systems, Manipal
Printed at Manipal Technologies Limited, India

www.penguin.co.in

For Deepak, Dhruv, Tara and Kabir

I stumble through this turbid life
I rummage through this sodden brain
I glimpse the gods go flitting by
I wonder if we'll ever meet

Contents

Contents

Acknowledgements

I am cognizant that there is a certain amount of impudence involved in writing such a book—as though one has all the answers. I am thankful to my editor, Manasi Subramaniam, who effectively eliminated all self-doubts and displayed confidence in this venture. It has been a pleasure working with her, and I appreciate that she was steadily prompt and precise in our correspondence. I especially enjoyed long conversations with my mother, Mira Gupta, who, no matter what, has always buoyed me with her pride in my writings. I am thankful to Dhruv, my son, for his suggestions and for patiently hearing me out despite his own tight schedules and deadlines. As for Deepak, I am grateful for him for just being there, always.

1

Introduction

If you want this, then do that.
If you want that, then do this.
Rules to follow
Rules to ignore
What life doles out
Is it in our control?

Us. We exist. We live in a quagmire of messy lives. We suffer through physical and emotional struggles. We propagate hurtful biases. We sully every compliment with suspicion. We brood, we fester. We resort to sarcasm liberally. We are miserly, we hoard, we wait endlessly for the perfect occasion. We never own up to being wrong. We rarely appreciate a gift. We wait for others to call. We are petty. We make do. We remain stuck in ancient regrets. We feel superior with inadequate knowledge.

We are directionless. We find daily lives a drudgery. We find fault with everyone and everything. Not today, not yesterday, not now and then, but always. We are completely convinced that this is going to be the story of our lives.

Them. They don't react when someone is rude to them; you rarely see them shout or slam doors. Even when confronted by a major setback, they withdraw, calibrate and turn the reversal to their advantage. They don't blame anyone for their misfortunes. Their compliments are genuine. They seldom make you wait for them. They know when to move away from an argument. They don't keep reminding you of the time you were mean to them. They forgive. They are curious about you. They don't go on and on talking about themselves. Even if you are to vent uncontrollably about someone, they will filter your conversation. They don't relish seeing you get in trouble. Their smiles, almost always, reach their eyes. They can laugh with complete strangers, they can make anyone laugh, they can laugh at themselves. They find fulfilment in things they have been doing every day. They seem to have a lightness about them.

Everyone would agree that there is a lot worth improving in the way we live and the way we experience the world. The moment of epiphany is when we realize that even we can become 'them', with studied effort. That we can remodel parts of ourselves and thereby change our lives. Yes, if we want, we can tweak this life. Merely believing this fosters hope and inspires us into action. This is a crucial acknowledgment that vast numbers of people are oblivious to. The very first step is to have the willingness to embrace a typology or, better still, a philosophy of change, to become open to change. This would mean to validate change by initiating self-transformation. In this regard, there are two main types of change. One involves familiarizing ourselves with certain characteristics within that are doing us harm. We can try to eliminate, transform or modify them. The second comes about if there is a sudden occurrence, good or bad, in one's life, and refers to the change that is required to live with these altered circumstances. Both types of change entail a proactive role to be played by the individual. This is a crucial life skill to adopt and embrace as it is increasingly apparent that those who adapt quicker, to either one of these changes or to both, can soften, if not eliminate, much agony in their life.

For many years, I found it intriguing to see the way our divinities are depicted while coping with struggles in their godly lives. There are different ways to explore this: through their appearance in iconic representations, literature, scriptures, rituals and myths. The source I have used in this book is mythology. Pithily, it is often stated that biography is about the life of humans and mythology is about gods. This is far too simplistic an observation. In actuality, myths are generally associated and have a symbiotic relationship with society. They are like a connecting chain, where communication between people from different ages is through stories embodied in the myths. In other cultures, myths are often relegated to a distant past. At best, they are used polemically to indicate an erroneous belief, or romantically to suggest an archaic or even sacred mode of discourse. However, myths, in the Hindu tradition, are very much alive and part of the ethos. They are narratives that endorse and empower our search for meaning through the ages. They are also simple and inviting stories that weave magic into the lives of people and creep into their very being, into their very essence, to be passed on from one generation to the other. Even though they are idioms of the imagination of the inner world, yet they bind, preserve, create a continuum—religious, social, philosophical and historical. The individual revelatory experience is also validated by getting incorporated into mythology.

Undoubtedly, some myths look like they are either meant to entertain or to symbolize a historical event. It seems that ultimately fantasy, history, reality and thought merge to create mythology.

Hindu mythology is humungous to the point of sometimes being unwieldy, partly because of certain unique traits it possesses. It is not static but dynamic, akin to a living organism, amoeba-like, growing and sometimes changing radically. Layer upon layer of history seems to have got assimilated in myths, which preserve traditions. Different myths mutate over the passage of time, with barnacle-like additions being made to them or truncations taking place in big and small measures. This is an inherent feature of the oral tradition, which evolves out of many combinations. This includes the Brahminical and the non-Brahminical voices. This gives birth to outstandingly curious and fascinating stories, which are constantly getting revamped. Since very little seems to get discarded, the result is a large storehouse of myths. The same myth may also have different versions geographically, with each region tossing out its own version of a story. This grand and yet inchoate nature of Hindu mythology could render one diffident in attempting to make sense of this veritable trove. Moreover, it is also true, when commenting on any Hindu myth, that there is always the risk that the opening of one vista may involve the closing of another. Yet, despite all these paradoxes, it is my understanding that mythology is a vast cultural resource for our perusal, free and easy to access. Anybody attempting to fathom aspects of the Indic ethos should make a beeline towards mythology. For this evolving tradition of myths is the intuitive, collective outcome of an ageless, nameless and diverse thought process. They are the keepers of our soul, so to say, and the keepers of many cultural traits.

Since myths have the capacity to resonate deep in the inner realms of our very being, they address common issues that we are in search of answers for. Some can leave us with a message that pushes us to reflect and sometimes even change our lives. This is, of course, only once we decode their metaphoric idiom and hyperbole. What excites and challenges me is that every so often the message cannot be encountered superficially. It is so embedded in the myth that it has to be carefully prised out. Then the next conundrum is that there is no singular, magisterial way to interpret them—there are no absolutes. There can be multiple simultaneous interpretations. Not to be straitjacketed, myths are an ebullient, buoyant source to work with, and an autonomous approach can be advocated for analysing them. Myths exists to give substance, not necessarily only to support moralistic behaviour but also to satisfy the psychological needs of believers. Some myths are undoubtedly parables but many are just reminders of the drama and richness of relationships and the vagaries of human behaviour.

I have looked at, studied, analysed and been enthralled by these ancient myths, unsurpassed in elements of scuffles, humour and beauty. By employing the messages I have teased out of them, I have attempted to use them for dealing with modern life: the everyday, the mundane, the unusual, the frightening life. I experience unrestrained glee when I think of the possibilities myths can offer. My purpose is to try and elevate the reader to a heightened feeling, to stir up emotion by welcoming them to insert themselves passionately into the narrative, ponder over them and look for new insights on how to live life.

Many a tumultuous event in the life of Shiva is recounted in the various Puranas. Shiva led a life of contradictions, unmitigated wonder and beauty. When faced with difficulties, he had to tread gently, take a deep look into himself, sometimes go against his inherent nature, and change, when need be. In the earliest and rather scant appearances, Shiva seems to have been a marginalized deity among the pantheon of gods, and yet he has become one of the most ubiquitous. Shiva, as Rudra, started off as being a silent, brooding sort of deity, but over the centuries, a spouse and two children were grafted on to his personality. The mythographers realized that they had to retain some of Shiva's earliest features, for the sake of authenticity, but there was also a need to expand his range. New myths were added, providing Shiva with additional traits, enhancing his repertoire and ensuring his survival in an ever-expanding celestial world. Sometimes, these traits clashed with his older image and gave rise to interesting scuffles, tussles and uneasy truces, that may or may not flare up, to provide new teachings as the millennia roll by. I have endeavoured to distil from the whole mass of Shaiva mythology a fine essence. In spite of this individual effort, as so many before, I am often stumped, for Shiva has the aura of an enigma, constantly baffling, constantly satisfying and constantly fulfilling the needs of followers through the centuries.

A group—to the uninitiated, a bizarre group—is depicted in artistic renderings, under trees amid rolling hills, with partly snow-capped mountains in the background against a golden evening sky. The scene is one of calm comfort and general contentment. Shiva and Parvati are seated on leopard skin, absorbed, preparing an intoxicating drink. Parvati is richly dressed while Shiva is resplendent in all the accoutrements of an ascetic. He has a detached yet comely look on his face, covered head to toe in white ash as snakes slither around his neck. A smaller figure on the side is that of Skanda with six heads, and yet another is of Ganesha, who has an elephant's head and the torso of a prepubescent boy. This is the most well-known celestial family, referred to as Shivaparivara—Shiva with his wife and two sons. The moment you think of a god with a family, you think of Shiva, with each eminent member of his family, holding a place in the hearts of devotees in and around the subcontinent and beyond. Shiva, the father of Ganesha and Skanda. Shiva, the husband of Parvati. Shiva, the son-in-law of Daksha. He truly has an actual family. Then there are the hordes of ganas who are inseparable from him, a family of followers whom he adores, and whose misshapen physical bodies are simultaneously a cause for mirth and deep philosophical understanding.

However, when we look at Shiva, in a clear visual sense, he seems to be verily clothed in the traits of an ascetic. Not just any old ascetic but a pronouncedly antinomian ascetic. He is a renouncer who is not supposed to have any interest in the family hearth and in everything that ties down a male member of Hindu society. His attributes of asceticism are unique and outlandish, to say the least, denoting a disregard for personal physical appearance, and a defiance and rejection of all socially sanctioned, literally man-made conventions and rules of conformity. It also represents a forsaking of all worldly activities and social participation while functioning as a dramatic marker of 'outsiderhood'. So, Shiva is the only major god known to be an ascetic. Therefore, he is not just a yogi but a Mahayogi. He has opted out; no mores apply to him as he leads the solitary and contemplative life.

Looking at this near-obsession with an overt self-governing world view, married life, with all its rules and regulations, doesn't seem to fit into the picture; yet, Shiva is happily married—not once, but twice. Sure, there are other married deities, but he is the only deity in the Hindu pantheon to have a family. In his persona, in his mythology, in his very being, Shiva straddles paradoxes, rendering him ambiguous, entertaining and a repository of life lessons, if one can see through the maze of contradictions. As a householder, Shiva does not abstain from the pleasures of the body or from the bliss of family.

What makes Shiva an ascetic when he enjoys all worldly pleasures? His asceticism seems to lie in his ability to control and regulate his mind and emotions. Shiva detaches himself and epitomizes introspection. We can see it in his encounters with other deities—he does not get into petty fights with Brahma or others over matters such as who is the greatest among them all. Instead, he comes to the rescue of deities when there is complete chaos and disorder. He is a stabilizing force because he has that power of mind which enables him to have the best of both worlds, materially and spiritually. Shiva represents how it is possible to be engaged outside and detached inside.

Modern conventional education, regretfully, does not focus on assisting the mind in different stages of growth, nor does it provide guidelines for transformation and preparation for all that life will throw at us. Yet, in order to lead the best life, it should be looked upon as one long process of evolution, gathering, along the way, skills we need to thrive, not just exist.

This book is a study of reflection, introspection and the necessity for taking responsibility. It is written with a conviction that genuine improvement makes one capable of mental feats that are useful in crisis situations. This book is about personal development. The caveat is that it will work when you integrate and make its teachings a part of your daily life. Micro improvements, that is, a few disciplines done every day, are enough to begin with, as taking small steps is more sustainable. Slowly assimilate what is being shared here and do not expect a miracle. Overnight success is a myth, going cold turkey has the aura of drama and bravery, but it usually does not last—it is not a viable long-term panacea. One cannot and should not even try to do everything all at once. Moreover, we often live with certain self-damaging quirks over long stretches of time, rendering them part of our cellular system, so to say. We are responsible for them hardening and calcifying into what seems like irremovable parts of our personality. So, keeping this in mind, grant yourself permission and a little indulgence to chip away at these foibles gradually, improve a little every day. This way, it does not feel like a major overhaul of what has become familiar, and yet every day, bit by bit, like homeopathy, there is improvement.

Recently, I heard someone say that each one of us is a mass of imperfections, and if we can recognize and live with our imperfections, basic nature, genetic defects and hereditary flaws, it makes for an easier transit in life's journey. The same person claimed that there are too many 'know-it-alls' in the form of self-help talks, books and programmes telling us how to live. In any case, the person continued, it is preferable to somehow stumble onto happiness. Sure, I thought, many will agree with this viewpoint with alacrity, grateful that they have a ready excuse to not take on the onerous task of working on themselves. But keep in mind, it is easy for a person who has achieved name, fame, money and who probably feels completely satiated with life to say this. This person, who scoffs at any attempt at self-improvement or development, obviously does not need any help. It may not be the case with several other people.

We have to, as individuals, take cognizance of the kind of life we want to live, the kind of person we want to be. We should not wait for someone else to design it. There are many individuals who attempt to do so by getting into a ruminative loop and starting the process of self-wrought change. 'Self-wrought' is key here, for we all know that being repeatedly reminded of a task by a querulous mother, a disapproving father and later maybe a nagging spouse is not always a motivating factor, rather it could have the opposite effect. Instead, you have to want it yourself. Let there be a need and a conviction arising from within yourself. Another caveat: as you proceed with the principles provided in this book, do not overthink, don't over-scrutinize. Let there be a balance. The very last warning: If you just want to go with the flow, without trying to change your situation, then this book, I am afraid, is not meant for you. But if you want to do an intervention in your own life, then by all means read on.

Adhyayan, that is, self-study, is to be practised all through one's life. It has been said so many times, by different philosophers from time immemorial, that an unexamined life is not worth living. Therefore, a penetrating look at ourselves, our values, our approaches and the invisible forces that shape our behaviour is non-negotiable. Most importantly, we must be sentient of all that we have gone through in our past. Abuse, abandonment, violence, poverty, death—all of these can negatively shadow us for a lifetime if we don't examine them and acknowledge them and the residue they left behind.

Anyone who loves the written word lives in anticipation of reading even a line that advances thought or evokes emotion. I, too, have a certain amount of hopeful giddiness merely envisaging the possibilities that may open up through the act of writing, which is exhilarating in itself. Yet, lest it appear like I have all the answers, that is far from the truth. I want to make it clear at the outset that I am not a psychologist and I have no training in the intricate workings of the human mind. What I do have, like many others, are some life experiences, some life observations and certain concepts and principles I have gleaned from them. My work on religion, for the past several decades, has often placed me in a privileged space where many people have felt comfortable telling me about their inner lives, so to say. I am grateful to those who have shared their experiences, discussing what they have gone through and how they have resolved conflicts. Additionally, I am constantly reading about gods and goddesses, the art, the icons, the prayers, which have all provided me with the ideas I have shared in this book. I have laid them out in six chapters as possible ways to lead a life and leave a life—when the time comes—with a sense of satisfaction rather than regret. My immodest goal is to also share the life of Shiva, as I have understood it, and relate it to our everyday lives in order to guide our transformation.

2

Ekagrata

Know him to be the supreme architect
Who is enshrined within the hearts of all.
Know him in the depths of meditation.
May he grant us immortality.

—Shvetashvatara Upanishad IV, 17

We are driven largely by the mind. The mind eludes, the mind deludes, the mind fluctuates, the mind agitates—the mind runs away from us, out of our control. It is as if the mind, though part of our corporal body, is an entity devoid of any interest in our well-being. It is not surprising that the mind is likened to a monkey that keeps darting about hither thither, playing tricks on us, making us do things, making us say things that lead to no good. It appears to be whimsical, flighty; everything points to the uneasy realization that the mind has a mind of its own! It has a power, which, if left unchecked, is capable of doing us harm. The solution lies in us not succumbing to it but harnessing it.

Ekagrata is a term meaning one-pointed, one-minded, fixated on a single point. It comes from the Sanskrit root word *eka,* meaning 'one', and *agra,* meaning 'proceed'. It refers to intentness on a solitary object or subject, undisturbed concentration and the pursuit of one matter.

Most people go on with life remaining oblivious to the power of their minds. Some of them are, gloomily enough, certain that they are not fortunate to be born with a worthy mind. Therefore, attempting to master the mind seems a waste of time. A second lot of people are convinced that destiny decides all things in life, so why waste time on monitoring the mind? These misconceptions have left many people apathetic about situations in their lives and seemingly bereft of any agency of how to change them. What I believe, firmly, is that the mind must be studied and eventually trained, structured, cultivated and calibrated. It will then have the capacity to work for us, in our favour.

A superficial glance shows that the mind seems to be nothing but thoughts and thoughts that repeat themselves—in Sanskrit they are called *vrittis,* or movements of the mind. This reminds me of that famous old song, 'Windmills of Your Mind', and the idea that thoughts are not getting anywhere but senselessly going round and round. Thoughts conceal in their labyrinth an unlimited chaotic flux. This mass of flux is fed by sensations, associations and memory, products of both time and milieu, and also conditioned by society. True independence, true freedom, comes to those who get acquainted with their thoughts. When thoughts are not examined and reflected upon, they can have disastrous results. They may be dramatic, they may be suspicious. Ekagrata stymies this 'thought monster' and acts like a psychic block, thereby putting an end to the dispersion and fluctuations of the mind and giving a firm unitary continuum. The striving should be to live with decisions and actions that stem from our clear-thinking mind. Defog the mind and act.

To arrest the 'psychomental' flux, the first step is to bring the mind under control. One way in which this can be done is to make it concentrate. Concentration, that is, *dharana*, comes from the root word *dhri*, which means 'to grip tightly', to hold fast. Through *nishtha*, or devotion to one ideal, and through *sankalp*, that is, firm resolve, one can attempt concentration by creating a stillness, a silencing of the internal dialogue—or one can say 'manylogue'— and then settling on one chosen subject alone. This is like doing a micro study. Anyone doing research day in and day out, working on one subject with steadfastness, would recognize the advantage of the complete mindfulness of ekagrata.

Meditation, the ancient life skill, provides us tools to deal with the mind phenomenon in an organized way and thereby achieve ekagrata. One must understand that life comprises both contemplation and action. Action is something everyone undertakes but quietude is seen mostly among truly successful people. More than ever, in today's time, where most people are perennially 'connected', it is a challenge to take out some non-action time. There is an art to meditation which can be learnt with relentless effort. It is called *dhyana* or dharana in the early texts, and is an important step and integral part of yoga. It can be said that it is the more advanced state, when the mind is concentrated on the object of contemplation without any break or disturbance, for a long time.

One could start by just sitting and not doing anything for a few minutes. These can be short periods of deliberately planned silences. In the beginning, it will be difficult and you will feel restless and itchy or just plain bored. By and by, it will become easier and you will discover a useful habit, which can be summoned when needed. In due course of time, one can sit in a particular posture: with the back straight and legs folded, in rock-like stillness with eyes closed, just concentrating on breathing in and out. One should attempt to move towards a close exploration of the senses, to an interior intimacy with the inner self. Where the mind is concerned, allow it to go rummaging, noiselessly. This is one way to exercise the mind muscles. Some may perceive 'quietening' the mind as being passive or not having much passion for life, but this is not correct. Meditation is purely an exercise to help the body and mind to rest in a state of perfect stillness.

There are many types of meditation but they all have the same objective: calming the mind by observing thoughts and emotions and centring the focus on one object. Meditation may not always have been part of the Indic ethos. Early historical times, rather, were redolent with animal sacrifices and fire worship. It is indeed remarkable that at one point of time some people became convinced that messy, senseless killing was not the means to experience release and fulfilment. Among other methods, they began pursuing meditation as an effective means of acquiring the knowledge that furthers self-realization, which eventually results in total freedom. To this day, meditation is extremely useful for achieving mental and physical good health and a sense of well-being.

Across the ages, and especially since the time of the earliest Upanishads—around 800 BCE—ascetics, contemplatives and sages have been grappling with consciousness to understand human behaviour and human nature. They were concerned with the structure of the human mind, wanting to see how far the conditioned areas extended and whether something existed beyond them. They studied obscure regions of the unconscious—the *samskaras*, the *vasanas*, the impregnations, the residues, the latencies, everything that makes up depth psychology today. They laboured over the unconscious in order to cauterize it.

Shiva is the supreme god that brings sharp focus to the activity of meditation, more than any other deity. He escapes from the chaos, isolating himself, and concentrates on an inner world. That seems to be a necessity for him as he has to deal with the myriad problems that keep cropping up in the celestial and earthly worlds. The image we get from Shaiva myths is that he epitomizes the concept of meditation entirely, and it is after practising immense mindfulness that he is able to help himself as well as everyone—the world, the universe, the very cosmos. After immersing himself in contemplation, he accumulates heaps of energy, both mental and physical, which help him deal effectively with issues. Each time he participates in strife, there is a corresponding depletion of his energy. Shiva, therefore, needs to periodically take recourse to solitary living. After aeons of meditation, the inward-looking Shiva comes out further enhanced.

That this is necessary is clear from the myths where the divine and semi-divine rush to him in times of apocalypse. Shiva steps out into the open, so to say, and knows exactly what action to take to dispel the harm. As a rule, he is not to be swayed from his meditation. It is true in the world of mythology that Shiva, if disturbed, is wrathful, and makes perpetrators suffer dire consequences. When Kama tries to strike an arrow of desire in his direction, Shiva opens his third eye, releases a missile of fire and reduces Kama to ashes. Yet, when beseeched by his fellow devas for guidance or support, if the need is genuine and his presence is urgently required, Shiva abandons his inner search and rushes to help, with full concentration on the job at hand.

This chapter will discuss the myths where Shiva literally closes his eyes to the material world. Immersed in contemplation, he is the ideal of poise, calmness and reflection. He is engrossed in *tapas*. Tapas is an archaic word which defines human austerities or techniques. It generates power in the practising individual and cleanses the mind, purging all memories and prejudices.

In ancient times, heat became a symbol of intense hard work, struggle and mortification. In mythological narratives, Shiva withholds all 'heat' inside his being so that he becomes a pillar of fire. Around him, nothing moves or flows, water becomes snow, all things become still. The world ceases to be. Countless sculptures of Shiva all over the subcontinent are representations of this very intense mental indwelling. The exceptional Mahadeva image at Elephanta in Maharashtra comes to mind—his eyes are shut, the look is inward, the half-smile lingering on the mouth denotes equanimity. The power of the image is undeniable; it has a serene beauty. Gazing upon it, you want to experience what he is experiencing.

Shiva's ability to focus and then use his stored-up power—gained from meditation—is interesting since it shows us exactly how a god derives such immense powers. They have to be gained by one's own striving. Shiva demonstrates feats of mental alacrity as a result of ekagrata.

Among the episodes in which Shiva is approached to save the world, the most popular is the *samudramanthan*, the 'churning of the ocean'. This incident has been written about numerous times, albeit with inevitable ubiquitous variations. The Adi Parva of the Mahabharata has a very elaborate version of this myth. It is also found in the Vishnu, Padma and Bhagavata Puranas. The mammoth dramatic act of churning has inspired beautiful visual art. Ancient and even modern art and sculpture often depict this episode in great detail, not just in India but through South Asia. The earliest pictorial narrative representation of this myth is from the Udayagiri caves near Bhopal in Madhya Pradesh. Here, the lintel at the entrance of the Gupta caves depicts the gods and demons tugging on the serpent Vasuki, coiled around the Mandara mountain. In later centuries, the churning scene also appears prominently in the Virupaksha temple at Pattadakal, Karnataka. In one of the latest depictions installed in the international airport in Bangkok, the devas, asuras, Kurma and Mandara are prominent, while Lakshmi's place is taken by Vishnu.

This myth, sometimes referred to as *amritamanthana*, is somewhat charming as one marvels how an inordinately mundane, daily household chore and mostly gendered activity is elevated to a stunning cosmic episode. From early times in India, churning is an important women-centric dietary activity. By churning milk, one thickens and refines it until it yields a richer substance: the precious ghee or clarified butter. Churning can be associated with purification as in the process of distillation the pure elements are brought to the surface. It is clearly drawn from a pastoral economy's everyday understanding of the importance and value of milk and its products. After all, it is not just water which is alluded to here; in the myth, the sea is a 'milky sea'. Ghee was and continues to be prized for all kinds of purposes, including medicinal ones. Similarly, the churning myth deals with the extraction of something pure: amrita. It also signifies a very important idea. Steeped in symbolism, it touches upon the theme of how creation proceeds from a body of primordial water where everything is formless and watery. Moreover, in this ocean water lies the potency or essence of life, variously referred to as *rasa, amrita* and *soma*. Only when this potency is released will creation begin. The milky ocean is also understood, metaphorically, as the ocean of consciousness and creativity which needs to be churned again and again to arrive at an understanding of the human condition.

In a remote past, the devas reside with the asuras in the heavenly world. The gods live in the constant fear that the world can be dominated by the asuras, and it is just pure physical might that keeps them at bay. The strength to keep the asuras in surly subservience comes with the regular quaffing of the elixir, amrita. But it has not always been the monopoly of the devas and sometimes the asuras get their hands on it. Once, the gods come dangerously close to losing their hegemony and absolute dominance over other creatures. With the asuras lying in wait for just such an occurrence, the devas begin to fret about this impending loss of control. In some versions of the story, we hear that the devas and even the asuras feel their power dwindling. In order to restore their strength, they have to immediately consume the elixir, what is probably referred to as soma in the Vedic texts and is now called amrita. The significance of this potion is that it bestows immortality and enables the gods to defeat the demons. It gives the gods the power to resume their *leela* and continue ruling over the world's desires.

However, a huge deluge floods and destroys the celestial world and drowns the amrita. In fact, the catastrophe also causes the loss of the goddess Shri, without whom the gods are no longer blessed with success or fortune; Kalpavriksha, the wish-fulfilling tree; Kaustubha, the ultimate jewel; Surabhi, the cow of abundance; and several other desirous items. The world is plunged into darkness, people become greedy, and no offerings are made to the gods. Indra asks Vishnu, the divine protector and preserver, to restore the universe to safety. Vishnu says to retrieve the amrita, the ocean has to be churned.

This is an enormous task and the very effort demands the colossal strength of titans. Prudently, the devas realize their incapacity to accomplish this alone, especially in their attenuated state. They sensibly decide that combined action is necessary. On reluctantly approaching the asuras, they have to agree to the condition that the asuras will receive half the quantity of the ambrosia. Following this transaction, they all proceed to the sea. Looking at the swirling ferocious waves, they are aware that they need to churn it, but where will they find an equally mighty churning stick? They decide that the sovereign Mount Mandara is eminently suitable as its magnificence measures 11,000 leagues with an equally astounding foundation underneath the earth. The devas feel that Mandara is also perfect as it is an empowered place, the playground of the *kinnaras*, apsaras and gods alike. It is dense with creepers and thickets, just like it is menacing with its resident beasts. But try as they might, the gods cannot uproot it without the help of Ananta. Once dislodged and carried to the sea, Mount Mandara, also called Meru, becomes the churning stick. All the divinities who can help out with the powers of their trademark characteristics chip in.

It is telling that Shiva remains absent from the collective eagerness of the gods to find the nectar of immortality. Actually, Shiva had not originally been a participant in this churning of the ocean. It is noteworthy that he is rarely ever a part of the skirmishes between the devas and the asuras. It seems Shiva, the Mahadeva, had no necessity to consume the amrita to be immortal.

Vishnu helps by manifesting in his avatar as Kurma, the tortoise, and goes to the bottom of the ocean to serve as a pivot for the churning stick. The king of snakes, Vasuki (also called Sheshanaga and Anantanaga), living in Patala, becomes the imperishable rope needed for the churning. Then, the asuras, holding the tail, and the devas, holding the head of the mighty serpent, pull to and fro, like humans playing tug of war, and start churning.

They churn for a thousand years. The sheer effort of it all makes the snake belch and release gas, which doesn't help the messy situation. The devas and the asuras are getting further drained of energy. Just when it seems like everyone will collapse with exhaustion, finally, treasures begin rising to the surface, among them gifts of prosperity and the best of animal, plant and mineral wealth. The gods, demons and other celestial beings scramble to claim the many riches.

However, in the midst of the great relief and pleasure, black smoke starts emanating from the ocean and spreads slowly but stealthily, like an evil giant, enveloping everything in its malodorous milieu. The devas and the asuras soon realize that it is a horrendously dangerous poison, *halahala*, also called *kalakuta*. Unpleasantly astonished at this turn of events, they begin to run hither and thither, coughing, gasping and frightened. At first, they are flummoxed and don't know what to do. Fearing for their lives, they gather in a large group and approach Indra once again. Vishnu has already helped as much as he could. On Indra's advice, the gods go searching for Shiva, who has great strength of mind and therefore a solution for many a sticky and prickly situation. Shiva has all the answers, Shiva Bholenatha is always ready to help.

Locating Shiva is never a difficult task, for if you search for him with all the hope, love and desperation in your heart, you shall find him, and they did. Seeing Shiva, tranquil and peaceful, deep in meditation, surrounded by foliage and being gazed at lovingly by Nandi and other ganas, they appeal to him. 'You, who knows all about the poisons of this world. You, who has poisonous snakes slithering up and down your chest, what do we do about this poison that will surely kill us all?' Hearing the quivering voices, Shiva slowly opens his eyes and sees the sorry bunch of divinities standing at a safe distance. You never know with Shiva, he may surprise you with his wrath. With hands folded, eyes beseeching and bodies bent in as obsequious a manner as possible, they recount, they lament, each one adding more and more gory details of their dire straits. Patiently hearing their plight, Shiva abandons his meditation and readily accompanies them.

When they return to the scene of destruction with Shiva, he calmly surveys the mayhem. The nervous gods are morosely standing on the sidelines, their eyes reddened, strained and watering. They cower, cough, spit, splutter, barely able to endure the foul smoke. There is blackness everywhere; the smoke is layering the trees, blanketing the land, enveloping the abodes. Confused animals dart about blindly, birds fly in all directions. Cupping his palm, Shiva gathers the foaming, frothing poison, and swallows it effortlessly. In one steady movement, the world is restored to normalcy. The gods, demi-gods and asuras heave a shared sigh of relief and barely remember to bow to Shiva as they once again begin scrambling for booty. Parvati, afraid that Shiva will be harmed by the poison, catches hold of his neck to prevent it from entering his stomach.

The poison leaves a blue hue on his neck, thus giving rise to the moniker Neelakantha, the 'Blue-necked One'. Some poems describe this dark blue stain as a blotch on his otherwise perfect neck; it may look like a deformity, but since it appeared due to compassion for his fellow gods, it is rendered beautiful.

This parable conveys the message that we must not get overwhelmed by bad experiences or allow 'poison' to spread in our mind and body. We must mitigate the impact of toxic situations and toxic people. Shiva, the absorber of all poisonous things in the world, does just that. He doesn't even need the nectar that the devas and the asuras are striving for, he already has the nectar—that is, the power of the mind. He draws his energy from the rigorous tapas he continuously charges himself up with. This stored power is what he uses to rescue the world. If we learn to conserve our energy, it can prove useful when we need it the most. The amount of energy differs from person to person. A person's energy might have completely depleted due to an unfortunate occurrence: the loss of a loved one, an adverse turn in business, or even a relatively mundane but enervating argument in the workplace. The loss of vigour and energy needs to be recovered, and the way to do it is spending time going inwards and meditating.

One can say that Shiva is the Destroyer as he destroys the poison. This is what can be called a 'constructive destruction'. At the same time, he is the Preserver, for does he not preserve the world? Incidentally, Vishnu, who is traditionally given the appellation of Preserver, was rendered helpless in the face of such a calamitous happening.

So when there is a crisis in our own lives, we hope that we can deal with it with equanimity. We hope that we will be able to call upon a state of lucidity. We encounter some individuals who have great clarity of thought. They know how to respond to the mundane, routine skirmishes of daily life and even the larger problems life exposes us to. Their minds seem to be in perfect sync with their actions and their speech. They have an aura of contentment and confidence. They know what they want and how to get it. This comes from coordination between their abilities and desires and also between their thoughts and actions. The power of their mind encourages them to strive for something they want. They have spent time exploring their thoughts and now know their inner desires.

Another myth illustrating Shiva's prowess to resolve a thorny issue revolves around the river Ganga. The kingly saint, Bhagiratha, needs water—not just any water but sacred water for immersing his ancestors' bodies for their ultimate journey. He decides to force his will upon the celestial powers and compel them to release the heavenly Ganga to descend and succour the earth. In his pursuit, he devotes himself to fierce and continuous tapas. Eventually, Brahma, pleased and enthralled by the ascetic's fervour, promises to grant a wish. Ganga agrees but is reluctant to leave her heavenly home and wilfully warns that being a mighty river, her immeasurable force, once directed to the earth, would decimate everything in its wake. Stuck now with the very real possibility of a deluge and unable to deal with Ganga's inherent nature, the celestial residents fuss over the future course of action.

The gods assemble and think it best to approach Shiva, the wise one, the helpful one, and the one with all the answers to complex situations. They go, once again, to Shiva as he sits in splendid isolation on a solitary summit of the Himalayas. There he is, steeped in pure and perfect meditation, absorbed in the crystal clear and supreme void of his own essence. Not without some trepidation, they implore that he should help them and the world out of this inevitable calamitous situation. Without much ado, Shiva acquiesces and gathers Ganga in his tresses; thus, suspended there, the world is saved.

Shiva carries a *jatamukuta*, a crown of hair on his head. His jatas are tangled, unruly and thick. Ganga, willy-nilly, has to make her way through this luxuriant growth, creating meandering partings as she tries to escape. Water, as we know, will always find its way to do what is in its inherent nature—to flow, to move. The mighty river divides into lesser streams, and Ganga's descent and subsequent arrival on earth is not only gentle but compassionate. She has been transformed. Ganga has to go through some tribulations to find herself while lost in Shiva!

Thus, it is Shiva's hair which becomes the saviour of the universe. Various environmentalists have looked at this myth as a strong message for the ecological chaos in the world. Shiva's hair has often become an important symbol of the forests which regulate the environment. His matted locks have been compared with the trees which control the flow of rivers and the rains and thus maintain the balance, thereby preserving the world. The myth has been translated in stone from early times. There are beautiful panel sculptures where Shiva is holding a strand of his hair to receive the heavenly Ganga in his locks. In calendar art, even today, his matted locks are spread open, and seen perched there is an image of a diminutive woman, Ganga. Once again, in this myth, the quick-thinking Shiva manifests his acumen to save the world.

I am fortunate to be a part of the teaching profession, where every day one can enter the lecture hall and share ideas and discourses with large groups of young adults. It is a world which requires continuous concentration, provided you want to connect and impact students, and not be just an indifferent professor. Increasingly, students are born into a culture of 'instant everything', where delayed gratification and patience are rarely encountered. The hope of the professor is to be not just coherent but eloquent, with thoughts translating into the right words, providing apt examples, with some humour thrown in. No doubt a certain amount of ekagrata is required to reach this goal for at least two hours every day. The experience of being completely immersed in what we are doing has been called as being 'in the flow'. It is a place of pleasure, delight and creativity, and gives rise to an optimal experience where nothing else seems to matter. Losing a sense of time is a good way of getting to know what we truly enjoy doing and what brings out the best in us. This is ekagrata.

My fellow lecturers have shared their own experiences of day-to-day stresses. I, myself, on some mornings, have been part of awful fights—especially as a young mother and wife—before leaving for work. It could have been with the spouse, the teenage offspring or just about anyone, leading to tears and harsh reactions. The intensity of the words exchanged and accusations hurled would put me in such a frame of mind where shutting myself in a room and crying seemed the only possible way to spend the day. Delivering a lecture would seem well nigh impossible as I thought I would not be able to forget the squabble. However, instead of brooding and reliving those harsh moments, I was thrown into a lecture hall with fifty-odd young adults, some respectful, some bored and some wanting to take you down. The ekagrata principle of focusing on the present moment and blocking out the recent past has helped me deliver more-than-satisfactory lectures, time after time. The lucidity in thought, knowledge and humour shared in the classroom makes me completely forget a rough morning, so much so that the ugliness of it all automatically reduces and the strength to cope with it multiplies. It sounds simple, tuning out the negative and keeping a one-minded focus on the job at hand, with no thoughts of anything else. It is doable, but it definitely requires practice.

The Katha Upanishad says, 'We always look outward and never look within: thus, we destroy ourselves. Only the courageous person looks within.' I spoke to several individuals who I consider successful human beings. Successful not just because they excelled in their chosen careers but because of other abstract, but to me important, signifiers. I questioned those who were able to maintain an admirable balance between the different aspects of their lives. Those who did not appear to get ruffled easily, those who had an openness and curiosity towards different ideas and behaviour. Those who were not self-obsessed, and, most crucially, those who didn't dwell on the sad aspects of their life, present or past, those who didn't constantly compare themselves with others or blame others for their present-day 'failures'. These were people I would consider successful from any angle. When probed, it was astonishing to find that the common denominator for all these people in different walks of life was meditation. They considered meditation one of the most important acts of their day. Some would do it twice a day, some for half an hour and others just for ten minutes. I am not surprised at this importance being given to meditation—right from the time we wake up in the morning till we sleep, we are busy verbally expressing ourselves, or are visually engaged in watching something. Even while out for a walk, we often have earphones on, listening to music or a podcast or just chatting with someone on the phone. This is also the case while driving. It seems we set aside no time to just be by ourselves. Negligible time is allotted to fortify the mind. Meditation can provide that time and structure. The intense mental indwelling that one experiences with its practice recalls the famous image of Mahadeva at Elephanta. This representation of Shiva is exceptional in its blend of vitality and repose.

Single-minded and regular meditation is taken like *sadhana*. This causes *atma shakti jagrithi*, that is, it awakens strength and speeds up the development of the personality, going by the belief that a treasure of untapped potential lies within us. It is an enhancement through inner alertness. Once encountered, these hidden capabilities may be used to the maximum.

Retiring inwards means spending time with oneself and pursuing self-knowledge and self-examination through introspection. We can get to know our aspirations and fears and whether we still want to pursue them. It is amazing to see how many people go about their lives not really knowing what they want. How can they work towards their goals if they don't know what they are?

Japa is a method which can help one experience ekagrata. It is the term for the repetition of a holy name, word, phrase or mantra. A mantra, a sound symbol, can be a single or a couple of words or even a syllable. It is considered powerful enough that when repeated it will bring about the desired objective. The idea of *mantrashastra*, that is, the philosophy behind mantra, is that every form has a sound and every sound has a form. A potent mantra can then be taken to be the audio manifestation of the deity. It is also supposed to align one's consciousness with the universal consciousness. It can be spoken in the mind, that is, in silence, or aloud. Formally, for spiritual progress, a sacred formula is selected by a guru for the worshipper according to their preponderant *guna* or quality—*sattva, rajas* or *tamas*. Then it is discussed and decided between the two whether the pupil would like to invoke his chosen god as a friend, guru, parent, servant, child or lover.

With a *mala* made of beads, stones or seeds placed in the right hand, a mantra is repeated. The beads are placed on the forefinger and the other fingers are used to move them simultaneously. The belief is that repetition causes the consciousness of the worshipper to be transferred to the deity or to the thought. The mantra is usually an affirmative pithy line.

In the habit of mala japa, one finds a beacon, a guide towards one goal. With the help of the mantra, one will attain mantra *chaitanya*, that is, mantra consciousness. The japa of a mantra can act as a fix, an infusion. During the japa, one is not doing any external activity but producing a sound, and the expression and reception of it becomes important. This sound will have some formulations, ideas and propositions, and if our intelligence begins to associate with the meaning of these things, then a mental intellectual infusion takes place which in turn nourishes and strengthens the mind.

The understanding is that power lies in the mere act of chanting. This is not surprising as, for the longest time, the oldest text, the Rig Veda, was not written down but transmitted orally from father to son over generations. In any case, reading a sacred verse is not the same as chanting it. This holds true even today, as many of us memorize lengthy prayers and recite them with feeling and the correct prescribed intonations. The belief is that since all mantras create specific vibrations, the words saturate our very being. What is required is faith in the mantra, which, when repeated for long, creates positive sensations that press upon the layers of the inner consciousness. Japa is done with the object of realizing the truth embodied in the mantra. It is also a voluntary focusing tool. The repetition of mantras has been compared to the action of a person shaking someone who is asleep to wake them up. The number of beads depends on your personal or religious preference—in the Hindu systems, it is usually 108.

I am aware of the latent power of japa. Repeating a combination of words so many times can convince us that something good will come of it. It makes one feel calm and brings about a stillness which increases concentration. I have found parents with restless children seeking advice about how they can make them sit still in class or even while doing homework. They are sometimes recommended the mala japa, with, happily enough, a satisfactory outcome.

Shiva, through meditation, also tries to destroy the ego within him, and hence emerges as a better god. The presence of ego in his personality traits might be there due to anger and passion, but through meditation, he emerges calm and self-contained. In another display of deep concentration, the gods are amazed to see the bliss Shiva emanates as he dances. His focus is paramount and its beauty undeniable. Meditation helps expand one's consciousness to such a height that all of life and its issues become bearable.

For ekagrata, multitasking is anathema. At one time considered a prized character trait, recent research has pointed out that it is not good for one's mental health to do many tasks at one time. Ekagrata is a life principle in which one concentrates fully on one thing. Though I do believe that, here, an individual should apply *viveka* or discernment, for there are certain chores you can multitask with. For example, surely one can fold clothes while talking on the phone. Or, it appears to be foolish to say, 'Hey, don't talk to me right now as I am cleaning the dishes.' But if you are concentrating on something really big, like planning a wedding or looking after a sick relative, it is best to try and give your hundred per cent attention. I find that those people who multitask regularly are the ones who have not brought about any worthwhile change in their character, for they don't have free space in their minds for deep introspection. They take great pride in their ability to do many things at once. They rarely sit still, let alone be contemplative.

Life shows us that we constantly have to make choices—which subjects to choose in school or college, whether to live in the same town as one's parents, whether to get married or not—and so we must also make creative adjustments to life. Most people move through life without awareness. Fettered by many desires which can never be satisfied, at every step we must use discrimination. By turning the mind inwards, one acquires the tool of viveka. It is best to meditate on life regularly, concentrate and study the options within the limitations. This becomes all the more important as it provides us with mechanisms for careful deliberation so we do not act hastily or rashly. But in order to succeed in this regard, stable attention is fundamental, and stable attention is developed by meditation.

We must question what we want and to what extent we are willing to go to get it. Ekagrata can help us discriminate, know the things we have control over and the things we don't. The mind tells us what to pay attention to, what can make us feel miserable, who we should spend time with, and who can cause us to feel sick with worry. It will be able to help us distinguish the correct way, in day-to-day matters and long-term matters as well.

The attempt is to instil ekagrata so we can lead a less agitated life, recognizing the principle that life is not all activity, movement or race; it is also contemplation, poise and absorption. I do believe that meditating and ekagrata leads to *laghutva*, a certain lightness of being, so to say. This is encapsulated in people who are unburdened by the swirls around them. We will be able to recognize them as they don't seem to carry any mental baggage; they are a sheer joy to be around. We may have an instant yearning to be like them. These are individuals who recognized long ago that their brains can focus better if they concentrate on one thing at a time. So, their attention while talking to us is flattering, to say the least. What sheer pleasure to have someone listen unwaveringly when you speak.

It is verily a science to understand and manage the mind. It is not a one-time activity, but, through *abhyasa*, that is, continuous practice, done steadily and regularly. It has been said in the Shvetashvatara Upanishad that the individual consciousness is a miniature, faithful representation of cosmic consciousness which is accessed by those deep in meditation. Lofty as it does sound to some of us habitual self-doubters, even we would agree that just contemplating such a possibility is truly a splendid thing.

3

Svabhava

> *O thou source of bliss!*
> *Poison is thy food*
> *Serpent thy garland*
> *Elephant hide thy garment and*
> *a big ox, thy vehicle.*
> *What then, wouldst thou give me?*
> *What hast thou got to give?*
> *Therefore, grant unto me only devotion*
> *to thy lotus feet.*

—Sivananda Lahari, Verse 87[1]

Sva means one's own and *bhava* is a condition or state of being. Bhava is a very significant word. It refers to several related matters—our outlook on life, our mental attitude towards all things, our particular reading of the universe, our state of ecstasy, our mood. All human beings have their own bhava. *Svabhava*—sva and bhava put together—means the natural state of one's constitution or one's innate, inherent disposition. Svabhava is our inscape, the unique essence or inner nature which is embedded in us.

I would like to stretch the scope of the word svabhava. So, let us suppose there are two aspects to it. The first, as mentioned above, is the internal—that is, our inherent characteristics, our behaviour patterns which emanate from our inner world, which, among other things, make decisions and help us function. The second aspect is the exterior—the instantly visible, 'seeable', outer appearance that we first notice when we encounter a person. This includes physical features, how one chooses to dress, and even body language. I would think the internal has a close bearing and influence on the external, as is illustrated in the case of Shiva.

In Shiva, there is a uniqueness of svabhava unmatched by any other god. In the external manifestation, it is abundantly obvious that he does not imitate any other deity; his complex innate nature constantly gets reflected in his exterior form, and his exterior svabhava is in sync with his interior svabhava. He presents a picture of wholesomeness to his worshippers. He is colourful, paradoxical and massively popular. He has a grandeur which is not complemented by expensive ornaments or beautiful, exquisite clothes. He has a grandeur of carriage wrought by extreme confidence. And his majesty lies in his individuality.

It is as though Shiva is empowered because he is in harmony with himself—he is comfortable in his skin, to adopt a very modern phrase. This is a more sustainable form of empowerment since it hinges on being self-reliant. This chapter will focus more on the artistic renditions of Shiva, found in icons, paintings and literature. Carrying mythic accretions and visual imagery, many of Shiva's epithets are found to compress a myth in a single frozen moment. For example, Gangadhar, Mahayogi, Neelakantha, Jatadhari and Chandrashekhara are some of the wonderful, visually explicit epithets that encapsulate elements of Shiva's personality, as elaborated in the myths, and can also be taken as a method by which he preserves his exceptional svabhava.

To study Shiva's svabhava, we will begin with a head-to-toe examination of his physical appearance and examine how far it corroborates his mental makeup.

Shiva seems to be verily clothed in the traits of an ascetic. Not just any old ascetic but a very antinomian unique ascetic. This is abundantly clear in his physical appearance, his personality, the very life he 'lived', and the way he is worshipped, even to this day.

Starting from the top, one of the first things that strikes you is the mass of hair on his head. It would be fruitful to bear in mind the significance of hair and how one chooses to dress it in certain cultures. More than ever, in the Indian setting, deliberate balding, endlessly growing, braiding, loosening or putting hair entirely in a turban, all have boundless symbolic significance. Shiva has wild, long, unruly hair, some of it spread over his shoulders, and the rest, as though hurriedly and uncaringly tied, in a bundled topknot. Jatadhari, Dhurjati, Jatin, Muktakesha and Kapardin are just a few of Shiva's epithets that mention his hair. Translated, they refer to 'one who has matted hair', 'one whose tresses are loosened' or one with 'coiled strands resembling snails'. Sure, this style of hair has been sanctified and euphemized when it is referred to as a jatamukuta, that is, 'a crown bearing matted tresses', but that doesn't take away from what can be considered a somewhat revolting way to arrive at this 'crown'.

Today, and no doubt from early times, the Naga Sadhus—Shiva's faithful clones—in their endeavour to be Shiva-like, have simply left the unshorn hair to grow and mat, either naturally or by dividing it into a number of braids in a rope-like manner. They ritually smear their jatas with a mixture of cow dung, cow urine, ashes and Ganga river mud, and can be seen rolling these ingredients into long strands. Loose hair, in many cultures, is associated with freedom. When Shiva chooses to mat his hair, it denotes a disregard for personal physical appearance, conveying defiance and rejection of society and all socially sanctioned, man-made conventions and rules of conformity. It also represents a forsaking of all worldly activities and social participation while functioning as a dramatic marker of 'outsiderhood'. It is a symbol of ascetic liminality. The dishevelled appearance also incorporates a sense of grief, mourning and despair for those still attached to the dead and the dying phenomenal world. So, it shows us Shiva's disregard for worldly customs but also represents his mourning for his dead wife, Sati. The outer explains the inner.

The myth that will be recounted here (see Chapter 2 for more details) indicates Shiva's svabhava of being calm and helpful. Ganga is a celestial river who has no desire to live on earth. She is forced to descend due to the arduous and severe tapas of the stubborn and astute sage, Bhagiratha. Grudgingly, she agrees, but petulantly warns her fellow divinities that the strength of her mighty and magnificent force would wreak havoc by drowning everything in its wake. It is Shiva's hair which becomes the saviour of the universe. Shiva gathers Ganga and places her on the top of his head. This is how Shiva got the moniker Gangadhara. In many images, we can see the diminutive figure of Ganga, mermaid-like, seated on one side of Shiva's head. His tresses are sometimes filled with other little symbolic figures—flowers or a skull. The flowers are of the Datura tree, from which an intoxicating drink is prepared. This is indicative of Shiva's fondness for this relaxing beverage. The skull is symbolic of death; it is also a common 'ornament' of the lesser divinities who constitute part of Shiva's retinue. However, more prominent and ubiquitous is a crescent moon perched precariously on the side or centre of Shiva's head, providing the raison d'etre for the appellation Chandrashekhara, 'the moon-crested one', and Chandrapala, 'protector of the moon'. The moon was procured by Shiva after the churning of the ocean. It has many meanings but it particularly symbolizes time, the lunar cycle, waxing and waning, and, by extension, birth and death. The moon seems to go through phases of birth, growth, fullness, decay, death and rebirth. Death is not the end for the moon; it is the prelude to a new beginning. The moon, thereby continually reborn, appears to have a power of renewal. Shiva is associated with this power, as his epithet Mahamrityunjaya, 'the conqueror of death', exemplifies.

Shiva's eyes are half shut in meditative thought. He also has a third eye in the middle of his forehead, which gives him the epithet Tryambaka, 'the three-eyed one', similar to other epithets such as Lalataksha, Vishalaksha, Trilochana and Bhalanetra—one who has an eye on the forehead. Fortunately for the world, this eye remains closed, for it is an eye of cosmic fire. Were it to open, its beam would annihilate everything in its way, as it did with Kama, who irritated Shiva when he was meditating. It seems that when the time is right, at the end of each era, Shiva burns the universe with a mere glance of his third eye. Another myth recounts how, once, Parvati playfully puts her palms over Shiva's eyes and instantly the whole world is plunged in darkness; hence, Shiva has to open his third eye.

Today's world has taken to the symbolism of the third eye generously. Among other things, the most obvious aspect is its ability to see and transcend the limitations of sense perceptions. In today's parlance, the opening of one's third eye is used to indicate sudden insight, like an intuition.

Where the mouth and lips are concerned, Shiva is almost always depicted with what is often described as an enigmatic half smile. There have been many interpretations of his 'smile'. It is aloof, seemingly unaffected by the tremendous display of his own energy. It appears to be the smile of one who is cognizant of the futility of all fuss. It is as though he is conscious of the secrets of the world, having grasped the effective path to contentment. The smile is filled with the bliss of self-absorption.

Due to his blue throat, Neelakantha is another one of those familiar and physically descriptive epithets. During the churning of the ocean, in order to save the world, he swallows poison, which renders his neck a becoming hue, not unlike that of a peacock. By this heroic saviour act, Shiva is graced by yet another epithet courtesy his endlessly grateful worshippers: Vishapaharana, 'the destroyer of poison'. This aspect of his outer svabhava shows another important feature of his inherent nature— fearlessness. There is a metaphoric message to his followers that, sometimes, one has to swallow poison in life, that is, miseries and sorrows—just like Shiva, these may leave their mark on us, on our memories, but we mustn't allow them to destroy us.

Whether Shiva stands tall or is seated in a yogic posture, he favours *bhasma*, ashes. He is depicted with a bare, ash-smeared chest. Tradition has it that Shiva first took to wearing ashes following the incineration of Kama from his third eye. Kama was trying to inflame Shiva with passion for Parvati, disregarding Shiva's activity of severe penance. Shiva irrefutably proved that the fires of yoga were greater than those of burning passion (*kamagni*). Ashes, like most things associated with Shiva, are a many-layered symbol, and have given birth to such significant theories that there seem to be a veritable theology of ashes. It is surprising, but due to its inherent nature, ash is capable of sustaining a number of implications. Besides fulfilling a practical function in giving protective warmth to the body, it has several other connotations.

Bhasma itself is variously understood, the most extreme of its meanings being the ash of dead bodies gathered from cremation grounds. It also means the ashes made by burning wood and cow dung. Shiva rubs the ash as an unguent on his dark body, which makes it appear luminous. He smears himself to remind everyone of the mortality of the body. When a person dies, the body can be destroyed by fire; what outlives the body is ash, which is indestructible. Ash is thus the symbol of the indestructible soul that occupies the body during life and outlives the body during death.[2] It symbolizes the complete mortification of the flesh, the triumph of the spirit over the world and the flesh, and the supreme detachment of all carnal desires.[3] There are many justifications given in the texts for this preference of something that is otherwise considered polluted and distasteful. As mentioned earlier, Shiva destroys the universe by a mere glance from his third eye by means of fire. He then purifies it by sprinkling it with ashes.

Ash is the vestigial substance that is created when things, beings and the material world are completely burnt off. In natural terms, it is the final state where nothing is left to burn, indicating the transience of all beings and the permanence of the supreme.

The ashes of human beings and animals, rich and poor cannot be differentiated. The diverse names and forms disappear and the real unity underlying all differences is attained. Shiva is the destroyer for he dissolves all diversities in the absolute unity. Everything can then fuse and blend. With no knowledge of caste or colour, everything is levelled in ash. Everybody's ashes are indistinguishable. Indeed, this represents the essence of all life. Ash is the symbol of matter which has ceased to be, from which the spirit has been released to freedom.

Shaiva devotees dress just like Shiva, or as close to him as they can be. Shaiva ascetics apply ash in the same manner as Shiva, while householder devotees apply *vibhuti*, that is, ash, from the *homa*, the consecrated fire where wood, herbs, roots and ghee are used to perform the ritual. Grey in colour, vibhuti is applied on the forehead. When applied in three horizontal lines, it is called *tripundra* and is the obvious sign of a Shaiva devotee.

Shiva is also considered to be the lord of the cremation ground; this is amply demonstrated by the large murals and sculptures of him at most crematoriums.

Shiva and his affinity to ash remind us to stay humble and remember the mortality that is each and every person's destiny, without distinction. Ash epitomizes the impermanence of life.

Shiva is Nagbhushan, the one who has serpents as ornaments. This association shows Shiva's power over dangerous creatures, most of all poisonous cobras. He 'wears' snakes as armbands and necklaces. He does not fear them. These snakes are the external insignia of his inner self mastery. Snakes are regarded as symbols of rebirth. They leave their old skin behind in the winter and hibernate until spring, when they return newborn. Akin to the moon, they are believed to be continually reborn.

Shiva's lower portion is wrapped in rough animal garb. His thousand epithets include Charmavasa, Krittivasa and Pashunama Patih, that is, 'he who is dressed in animal hide'. One may ask, why animal hide? Does he hark back to a human phase in antiquity when such attire was commonly worn due to a need to camouflage, to beguile prey, as a hunter? Indicative of his forest-dwelling antecedents, the animal garb could be the skin of a tiger, leopard, an antelope or even an elephant. He thus gets the epithet Gajasura, 'the destroyer of the elephant demon', a sign of his victory over the demon of false pride. An elephant's skin is crumpled, full of fat; it cannot be tanned and used as leather. In artwork, Shiva is usually shown in tiger skin or deer skin as these are probably easier to recognize—with their stripes or spots—compared to an elephant's skin.

This animal attire could also be to signify his quality of being close to animals. Pashupati or 'the lord and protector of animals' is another of his popular epithets.

As for the tiger skin that he is said to wear, the myth relating to Daruvana tells us that the rishis create a tiger to attack Shiva, who is disturbing more than just their peace of mind. Shiva slays and dons the skin of the tiger as a trophy. Devadaruvana, similar to Darukavana, is geographically placed close to the western ocean, but another *vana* of the same name is found near the Himalayas near Badrinath. It seems here that sages, accompanied by their wives and sons, perform penance with sacrificial fires. Though Shiva is delighted, he wants to test their sincerity and turn their minds from observance of sacrificial rites to the path of renunciation. Thus, in order to test their faith, and sportively too, he assumes a deformed but attractive form. He is nude and dark in complexion and has three eyes, but even in this form is extremely captivating—smiling and singing and moving his eyebrows seductively. He creates sensual feelings in the hearts of the women, that is, the seemingly virtuous wives of the sages, who start following him with great enthusiasm; stopping all activities, they gather at the threshold of huts and seem not to care that their garments and ornaments are loosened. Their eyes start rolling due to excitement. Even old women beyond the age of seductive charms begin to display amorous gestures. Some, with waistbands dislodged, begin to sing. One of the Brahmin women is unaware that her upper and lower garments have slipped off. Everyone is so mesmerized that some cannot distinguish between their kinsmen and the multi-branched trees. Falling, they roll around on the ground as others dance. One lady lies on the ground like an elephant and begins to talk loudly. Soon, they embrace each other and talk to Shiva: 'Who are you? Sit. And where are you going? Be pleased with us.' Tresses dishevelled, even chaste women fall down due to his maya in the most awkward postures in the presence of their husbands.[4]

Then the angry Brahmins start saying harsh words. Their powers of austerity are ineffective against Shiva in the same manner of the lustre of stars in the sky against the refulgence of the sun. They realize that this is a great persona and begin to question Brahma. They are told that they need to show devotion to Shiva and that detailed sacrifices are of no use compared to true steadfast devotion. In any case, Brahma says, 'O Brahmins, never should a guest be dishonoured by the householder even if they happen to be deformed, dirty or illiterate.'

This is also Shiva's nature—to test devotees and teach them, through his playfulness, important lessons of life. Clearly, his intrinsic nature is in fluid relation with the exterior. He is fearless, unbothered about people's opinions. He is autonomous. He makes his own rules. He believes in the equality of life forms, and considers nothing low or polluted. Though inherently an ascetic, Shiva changes his svabhava by getting married when the need arises, thereby changing his inherent nature.

We can get to know our svabhava by taking a close look at ourselves from time to time. This can be achieved by spending some time in solitude, exercising naked, raw honesty, and tackling some tribulations. For it won't be a piece of cake to be self-reflective and to not deceive oneself of one's weaknesses and strengths. In other words, uneasy truths must first be confronted and then worked upon. Many a time, habits appear to be unshakeable. It is an uphill task to rid oneself of them. But the positive outcome of studying oneself is that such reflection will draw attention to our many foibles.

The key word here is honesty. Many people do not care to spend time with themselves or churn their minds honestly, almost brutally, to realize what it is that they actually want. Some people claim they do, but in reality, they don't. This is evident since they continue to live with the image they have created of themselves in their own minds, which flatters and pleases them but is not necessarily who they really are. So, it cannot get them to their desired goals. We all know our positive traits. It is usually the negative traits that elude us. Entire lifetimes go by and we don't realize if we are self-centred, miserly, arrogant, judgemental, sarcastic, touchy, insulting, annoying or even lascivious. Then, we are so self-righteously astonished when somebody, in a fit of irritation, tells us so, and we promptly decide it is because the person is jealous, and we don't look at this as an opportunity to introspect. If we are honest, maybe we can do something about what they have pointed out. Knowledge of ourselves can be ruthless; to be in an illusion, a self-created bubble, is the simplest path.

Another method to know your svabhava is through the thoughtful intervention of someone you are close to. That person can see what you actually are and gently point it out to you. Sure, it will be hurtful, maybe even shocking and difficult to digest. However, once you get past all that, you will empathize with the person who had to gather courage and risk all to be honest with you in the first place. You will be grateful and begin the process of change.

I always feel that if you truly love someone, their damaging features should be pointed out. This requires great fortitude. Many a husband, preferring not to open the proverbial can of worms, has zipped his mouth shut and never told his wife that she is quick to judge, or just not fun to be around, or that she is too busy being a mother and has wilfully abdicated the qualities he first fell in love with. Similarly, many a wife has chosen to 'keep the peace' by overlooking her husband's indifference to her cooking skills, her appearance, or even his lack of imagination while making love. Grouses get stacked up, albeit silently. Temporary escape routes are sometimes taken via a separation or an affair, or the couple may continue to live in this manner, spreading the dreariness of the relationship. We have all seen couples with this vapid aura lingering around them. They can be seen sitting across each other in a restaurant and barely exchanging a look, let alone a word. It is remarkable how many partners can go on living like this, year after year, not sharing what is going on in their minds—good, bad or ugly.

When we sit back and introspect, we must ask ourselves a lot of questions. Am I happy with what I have? If not, then what do I lack? Am I working towards accomplishing or acquiring it? Am I taking the right steps? Are they practical? So, when we undertake this analysis, we become transparent to ourselves. When we are truthful with ourselves, we can find ways to change or rectify a situation. Each of us has to ponder and become conscious of our own svabhava.

There are two things we must keep in mind. First, we must understand our inherent nature. We must recognize the good and the unwholesome in ourselves—embrace self-acceptance and practise no self-deception. It is damaging when others delude you into believing something detrimental, but what can be worse than deluding yourself, and throughout your life not recognizing what your actual traits are. We can also easily fool ourselves and take the great self-deception route, believing that we are good enough as we are and there is no need for self-improvement.

One method of understanding your svabhava is looking at your personal history. Past damages have to be addressed. Were you abused as a child? Do you have any severe complexes? Have you not been able to move on from the death of a family member? Think about what you need and should do with your life to clear these latencies, for they would almost certainly have impacted your inherent nature. Believers of Hinduism speak of latencies from a past life that can cause harm if the right rituals are not performed, but the ones in this life are far more crucial to your sense of well-being. Don't be passive if they are stopping you from leading a joyful life. Maybe you can speak to a professional. Try hard in any which way to move on. These 'bad things' are in the past. You probably had no control over the situation as you were either too young or helpless. Try and have some control now, over patterns that have emerged due to your own personal history.

The next step is to see what doesn't work for you, what trait of yours does not serve you well considering your own nature. It is my firm belief that svabhava is inherent but not immutable. It can be changed depending on what you want to do with it and how you approach it. Let us say you are a perfectionist. You feel like the world has come crashing down if there is a disturbance in the decor of your home or a delay in an appointment or your outfit for the evening has become imperfect due to a stain. You are stuck on what you consider the big picture but actually it is not. Your perfectionism, which you consider an admirable trait, is slowly killing you. Not only do you lose sleep over minuscule things but eventually your health is affected, and probably your relationship with friends as well. Only the wise will excavate their true nature from the deep recesses of their being and allow it to be examined. In many cases, it remains dormant, not unlike a sleeping monster.

You will be able to see this stagnancy when a person stays unchanged after decades, inherently and outwardly. The premise is that we are responsible for what we are and whatever we wish to be in the future. The sum total of what we are today is, after all, the result of the past. Similarly, we can 'construct' our future selves since they will be a result of our actions today, so we must act as soon as we realize that the choices we make are up to us. We have the power. Science has recognized that human beings have the capacity to change. Stories abound from our literary heritage to illustrate this. Valmiki transformed from a hunter to a Sanskrit scholar-poet, writing with immeasurable and everlasting beauty. Angulimal was once a ruthless dacoit and then became a believer in ahimsa, a Buddhist. Tulsidas, earlier an ordinary man, prey to his degrading lust, also became a wonderful poet and gave us the 'Ramcharitmanas'. Nothing is cast in stone. Brain patterns do change over time in response to our thoughts and experiences. That is why we constantly hear the phrase, 'be positive'.

The other way to get to know one's svabhava is far subtler and requires a willingness to take note of how the world responds to us. Sometimes, people's remarks towards us or their attitude—spoken and unspoken—can give us valuable insights and also be a trigger or a catalytic agent to change damaging behaviour. For instance, we might find people are trenchant or reticent in our presence, keeping a sullen silence when we are around. Yet, the same people could be garrulous and jolly with others. We just have to notice these indicators.

It took a while for me to get to know myself—it is not a one-time affair or a static process. It may appear to be an exercise in excessive self-absorption, but in the larger scheme of things, all the people surrounding an 'awakened' individual will benefit with the clarity that is achieved. We need to sit by ourselves and see what works for us and what we are comfortable with. We all have to be clear about what we want to create in our lives. For, when we try to be like everybody else, we blindly follow the rules, whether they suit our inner nature or not. As a consequence, we do not emerge as authentic human beings but just bad copies of other people. This eventually causes conflict. Some people may 'appear' comfortable in following the rules, and that is fine as well. If you are dissatisfied with the way your life is going, do introspect and observe the qualities you have within you and identify which of them are unique; then move towards honing these unique skills. By doing this, you can develop your strengths, which will enable you to put lesser effort towards greater results. Be cautioned that your calling must reflect the shifting, changing light of life. As and when circumstances shift, we can reflect on the changes that have taken place in our inherent nature and proceed accordingly.

From dressing a certain way to developing a certain style, everything stems from how well we know ourselves. Whether it is the kind of lifestyle we should strive for in order to be successful, or the friends we need for a 'happy' life, it is amazing to see how people get convinced that certain suggestions are often of the 'one size fits all' variety. Yes, you may not be toeing the line, you may not be walking the beaten path, but you will have an inner satisfaction of doing what agrees with you the most. Do not be afraid to be different. As the idiom goes, 'March to the beat of your own drum'—as a unique individual, you need identity, you need significance. If you don't find the right way to feel significant, the sheer desperation to fulfil this need might even propel you towards harmful ways.

We shouldn't try to copy others as this will adversely impact our genuineness, which may cause conflict and lead to frustration. Instead, aspire to be the best you can at whatever you choose, in accordance and in tune with your svabhava. However, even this principle does not have to be carved in stone. There should be a recognition that you are allowed to change your mind, whether it is in the area of relationships, career or any other space.

When we blindly follow instructions, we ignore the individuality of a person. We forget that each individual is born with certain traits. It took a while for me to realize what my boundaries are. This came with clarity, which in turn came with practise.

It is far better to develop abilities of our own which have come from our own encounters with life. Each of us has some impregnations which come to define our personalities. We all have our own personal history, so to say. Maybe, for example, someone has had an impoverished childhood and their needs and frustrations differ from someone who has had an economically better life. People are scarred in different ways. We should look inwards and get to know this inner self, understand our own behaviour. This will ultimately lead to contentment.

We should have the courage and patience to find our own calling in life. This is the true, real meaning and the idea behind personal autonomy. It lies in realizing and cherishing our personal choices when we can. Everyone should pursue their own sense of self and recognize that each individual is different, and in this difference and variety lies the beauty of life. Each person has their own level of energy and potential, and that should be maximized rather than wasted by trying to become something else.

More importantly, when we learn our true svabhava, we will cease to envy others, due to the realization of the futility in trying to go against our inherent nature—we experience contentment just knowing that someone else's life is not suitable for us.

I have often wondered why it is considered such a compliment when people say you haven't changed. When they are talking about physical changes, I can perhaps just about understand—it means you haven't aged, which, sadly, to many individuals is the only concern in life. However, when they are talking about your character, I do not think it is a compliment at all. I would prefer to be recognized as an evolved and better version of myself. I should hope we all change over a period of time. Very few of us can claim to be born as paragons of perfection with no scope for improvement. There are poems and songs in which composers claim they don't want their beloved to ever change, and it is said that the ultimate manifestation of love is to love a person the way they are, not the way you want them to be. However, realistically speaking, some traits that are endearing and charming in the early years of a romance can jar and become repugnant over time. Life demands that we be vigilant about the differing circumstances in our lives and our milieu and make the required adjustments. Some tweaking is always desirable. I would love to start a campaign to refashion the exclamation 'you have changed!' into a positive way to greet someone.

I have learnt from Shiva to develop a distinct style of attire and not change due to an arbitrary fashion trend—everything does not look flattering on everyone. It can change from time to time because your body shape has changed or because comfort is now higher up in your priority list.

So, firstly, we should not just be part of the herd, but have our own unique qualities. Secondly, we shouldn't simply lust after the qualities that someone else possesses unless we are ready to make the leap to change ourselves. Since change is the law of nature, it should not be something we dread. It is true that most people resist change and want to maintain the status quo as they get comfortable with the passage of time.

We should accept ourselves and embrace and celebrate our own uniqueness until the time that it serves us. When we are envious or we feel like a lesser person, we must catch ourselves and stop the 'I am like this only' lament. Don't live up to others' expectations or become a clone—be what you desire to be. Like us all, Shiva had an inscape, but he also had to give in to others at times. He was not rigid, and made compromises when he deemed it necessary. Even though his exterior form did not undergo major changes, he did change his basic svabhava of being only an ascetic and got married when the circumstances demanded. He also dealt with the consequences of his temper by learning to control it.

Shiva went on to occupy a commanding position on celestial as well as earthly terrain. Therein lies the beauty and marvel of Shiva: He is accepted, loved and worshipped by his devotees, with all his mutations and peccadilloes.

4

Samarasa

Shiva shakti yukto, yadi bhavati shaktah prabhavitum.
—Saundarya Lahari, Verse 1[1]

[Shiva, united with Shakti, becomes able to manifest.
If otherwise, this god knows not even how to pulsate]

Sama means equal and rasa is essence and bliss. So,
samarasa refers to equal bliss. It means having a kind
of equipoise or 'equal feeling', in a manner of speaking,
being in a state of harmony and non-discrimination. For
me, and for the purpose of this chapter, it translates as an
ideal relationship with a partner.

In our 'religiosphere', the majority of dominant deities
are couples: Sarasvati and Brahma, Sita and Ram, Radha
and Krishna, Lakshmi and Vishnu, and, of course, Parvati
and Shiva. We clearly have a preference for twosomes and

like to see our gods married, or at least with a partner. To further validate this point, there are epithets that consist of conjoined names and give prominence to the spouse, as is seen with Shiva. In various epithets where his wife's name significantly appears first, he is Girijapati, Umamaheshvara, Bhavanipati, Umapati and Gaurishankara, to cite a few. These names illustrate the importance of the coupledom that Parvati and Shiva share. The two appear vividly alive, more than any other pair, in myths, regional stories and art. It is truly remarkable how very riveting this relationship is, and what an actively communicative couple they are.

Sati is Shiva's first spouse, and with both his spouses, he has memorable exchanges and dialogue, illustrating the caring, sharing, quarrelling and forgiveness evident in these associations. What also gets manifested is the tension between egos and the very dialectics of a relationship that strives for equality and acceptance. They discuss, listen, talk and compromise. The salubrious nature of marital squabbling is shown constantly in Shaivic myths. The fights are remarkable, where both parties threaten, browbeat and try to convince each other so that they can, eventually, come to a rapprochement.

So, Shiva's induction into marital life was through Sati. The Satikhanda of the Rudra-Samhita in the Shiva Purana elucidates this union in great detail. Sati takes birth to beguile and compel Shiva to fall in love with her. Shiva's asceticism is a perennial problem for the gods; if he remains detached and refuses to take a wife, how can auspicious creation come into being? Therefore, Brahma and Narada also plead with Sati to take Shiva as a husband. Validating her own need, Sati combines it with the existential cosmic urgency. Eventually, it will be seen that Sati plays the role of mediator and succeeds in involving the ascetic god in creation by transforming him into a god of great sexual power and vigour. This is her triumph.

Her birth is marked with all the auspicious omens befitting one with such a momentous task ahead of her. As a small girl, while engaged in various sports with her girlfriends, she draws pictures of Shiva every day.[2] Whenever she sings sweet songs, as is usual in childhood, she remembers Shiva.[3]

Once she blossoms into a young woman, her beauty blazes forth brilliantly.[4] Her desire for Shiva grows every day. She approaches her mother and seeks permission to perform penance with Shiva as the goal. Firmly resolved in her desire to secure him as her husband, she propitiates him in her own house. In the month of Ashvin in September–October, on the Nanda *tithi*s, that is, the first, sixth and eleventh days of the lunar fortnight, she worships Shiva with great devotion, offering cooked rice with jaggery and salt. She spends a month doing this. On Chaturdashi, the fourteenth day of the month of Karttika in October–November, she worships and meditates on Shiva, offering sweet pies and puddings. On the eighth day in the dark half of Margashirsha, November–December, Sati worships Shiva with cooked barley and gingelly seeds. On the seventh day in the bright half of Pausha, December–January, Sati spends the night keeping awake and worshipping Shiva in the morning with cooked rice and *krishara*, jaggery mixed with gingelly seeds. She stays awake in the full-moon night of Magha, January–February, and worships Shiva on the banks of the river, wearing wet clothes. On the fourteenth day of the dark half of Phalguna, February–March, she stays awake in the night and performs a special worship of Shiva with *bilva* fruits and leaves every three hours. On the Chaturdashi day of the bright half of Chaitra, March–April, she worships Shiva with *palasha* and *damana* flowers day and night. She spends the rest of the month remembering him. After worshipping him with cooked barley and gingelly seeds on the third day of the bright half of Magha, January–February, she spends the month consuming milk products obtained from a cow. After worshipping Shiva with offerings of clothes and Brihati flowers on the full moon night of Jyestha, May–June, she spends the whole month observing a fast.

Now that Sati is ready, Vishnu joins the other devas and they all go to Shiva. They sing his praises for a long time, and once he is pleased, he asks them what they have come for. They tell him that they are not able to do their duties as there is one particular demon who can be destroyed only by Shiva's son. Therefore, for the sake of the universe, they implore him to take a wife. They tell him that like Vishnu has Lakshmi and Brahma has Sarasvati, he must also get married. Shiva tells them, 'O best of devas, it is not proper for me to marry as I am detached from the world and engaged in penance. I always practise yoga. Of what avail is a beloved for me in this world since I am in the path of abstinence, delighting myself in my own soul, freed of attachment, unsullied, with the body of an ascetic, possessed of knowledge, free from aberrations, and a non-reveller. Besides, I am always unclean and inauspicious. Hence, what can I do with a beloved wife? Even as I am engaged in yoga I experience mystic bliss. Only a man devoid of perfect knowledge will make much of marriage and desire it. Actually, it is a great bondage. Hence, I am not interested in it. This is truth. I am telling you the truth. None of my activities is pursued with self-interest. Yet I shall carry out what you have for the benefit of the universe.'⁵

Shiva gives in and asks them to suggest a woman with comely features who is familiar with yogic practice and would be able to receive his virile semen in parts. She must be a yogini when he practises yoga and a loving woman when he indulges in love. Shiva says he is always subservient to his devotees. But he has two conditions: 'When I go into a trance, O Brahma, in that meditation, damned be she who causes an impediment therein . . . It is this worry that kept me unmarried, O Brahma. Hence, get me a wife who will follow my activities ever. There is another condition: If she evinces a disbelief in me or what I say, I shall abandon her.'

Sati has already done severe penance, and due to her great devotion, Shiva tells her to ask for a boon. She makes it clear to him, albeit in her shy way, that she desires to be married to him.

This is how Shiva becomes a householder and indulges in noble dalliances.

Daksha, Sati's father, had been meticulously and studiously arranging spouses for his countless daughters. They were married off to gods and important personalities. His most beautiful, most intelligent and favourite daughter is left, and before he can choose a suitable spouse for her, alas, she chooses Shiva, the wild wanderer who smears ash on his body and is primarily an ascetic with matted locks and snakes adorning his chest, and no interest in matters of matrimony. He refutes the prescribed order and is the master of his own will. When the nubile Sati wants to marry him, Daksha, the epitome of caste and class hierarchy, is aghast at her choice and rejects the match right away. Here, we can see a classic relationship of disagreement and scrimmage between father-in-law and son-in-law. Daksha's dislike for Shiva originates primarily from the fact that Daksha is a faithful follower of Vishnu. If you adore Vishnu, there can be no room for a Shiva-like god. This bespeaks of a historic cultic tension between the two major divisions of Hinduism. Moreover, Shiva's behaviour is far too outlandish for Daksha to stomach. Shiva does not care about Brahminical norms or anyone's opinions, and had moreover insulted Daksha at a gathering.

Despite the father's grave misgivings, Sati eventually has her way and gets married to Shiva. Daksha is left silently seething, helpless in the face of what appears to him to be his daughter's despicable, unfathomable infatuation. Fortunately, the couple shares a very amorous and happy marriage. Once they reach Shiva's abode in the Himalayas, the scene is so beautiful that it renders Sati speechless. The summit shines with lakes and forests and has variegated colours of various gems. It is embellished by lotuses of diverse forms, shapes and lustre. It shines like the rising sun, abounding in crystalline clouds and sparkling with grassy plains and plenty of trees. Flowers are in abundance and boughs of the full-blown and blossomed trees are surrounded by humming bees. Various birds such as the chakravaka, kadamba, swans, geese, intoxicated sarasa cranes, peacocks and male cuckoos can be heard. Many kinds of semi-divine beings like the Ashvamukhas, the Siddhas, of great purity and holiness, the apsaras and the Guhyakas roam there. Their womenfolk—the *vidyadharis*, kinnaris and mountain lasses—play about here and there. The celestial damsels play on their lutes, tambours and drums and dance with enthusiasm.[6] These sporting times are full of ardour.

Shiva's first and most important task as a married man is ensuring privacy. Recalling how it was when he was single, with the ganas freely going in and out of his home, he now summons the blissfully happy Nandi and his other eager attendants. Shiva tells them, in as many words, that they are not to approach him unless requested.

Then, Shiva transforms from the perfect ascetic to the perfect lover. He gathers sylvan flowers, making wreaths and garlands and putting them around Sati's neck. When she is admiring herself in the mirror, Shiva approaches her from behind and peeps at himself too, just to get close to her. Sometimes he plays with her earrings. At other times he applies red dye on her already reddish feet, rendering them even redder. Even when something can be said aloud, he whispers it in her ear in order to see her face closely. He never wants to go far from her and returns fast if he does go, putting his hands over her eyes and asking her to guess his name. He makes marks like bees on her breasts that resembled the buds of a golden lotus. He removes her bracelets, bangles and rings one by one and then puts them back on. He does not carry out any activity without her and is not happy away from her side even for a moment.

In the ridges, caverns and grottos of the Himalayas, they cavort endlessly. Drinking the nectar from her moon face, he is bound to its sweet fragrance, her beauty and her jocular pleasantries, just like a huge elephant is bound with ropes.

Ten thousand years go by and Shiva travels from place to place, even visiting Mount Meru, other continents and different forests and parks. Even though he goes to such faraway places, he always returns home to Sati as it is only with her that he finds peace and pleasure. He gets no pleasure from sacrifices or the Vedas or penance.

Day and night, Sati stares into the face of Shiva and he, the great lord, stares into the face of Sati. Thus, by their mutual association, they nurture the tree of love.[7] After sporting about like this till she reaches a state of satiety, Sati becomes less attached. One day, after delighting the lord with her devotion and obeisance, she says, 'O great lord of lords and ocean of mercy, O great yogin, the uplifter of the distressed, take pity on me. You are a great Purusha, the lord beyond sattva, rajas and tamas. You are both Saguna and Nirguna. You are a great lord, a cosmic witness, and free from aberration. I am blessed since I became your beloved wife, sporting with you. O lord, you became my husband because of your love for your devotees. O lord, after sporting with you for so many years I have become fully satiated and now my mind is turned away from it. O lord of gods, I wish to know the great pleasing principle whereby all living beings surmount worldly miseries in a trice.' She wants him to explain that activity which enables people to obtain the supreme region and free themselves from worldly bondage.[8]

Shiva explains to Sati: 'Know that the perfect knowledge is the great principle, the consciousness that "I am Brahman" in the perfect intellect where nothing else is remembered. This consciousness is very rare in the three worlds. O beloved, I am Brahman, the greatest of the great, and very few are those who know my real nature. Devotion to me is considered the bestower of worldly pleasures and salvation. It is achievable only by my grace.[9] There is no difference between perfect knowledge and devotion. A person who is engrossed in devotion enjoys perpetual happiness, and that is why because of it Shiva even goes to the houses of the base-born and the outcastes. Knowledge (*jnana*) and detachment (*vairagya*) have grown old and have lost their lustre in the Kali Age. They have become decayed and worn-out as the people who can grasp them are rare.'[10] Shiva goes on to explain to Sati the benefits of devotion, that in this age it has immediate and visible benefits. He is subservient to a devotee in view of the power of devotion. True devotion is as endearing to him as to the devotee.

Later, Sati enquires about virtue and righteous living and the sacred lore of the Yantras and Mantras. Shiva is so delighted with her interest in all these matters that he tells her legendary stories of the greatness of the votaries, the norms of people of different castes, the stages of life, the duties of kings, sons and wives, medical lore, and even explains the science of palmistry.

Sati's life appears to be bountiful and beautiful. She clearly enjoys sensuous and intellectual fulfilment. However, as it happens—what every young bride should be cognizant of, but sometimes isn't—just a husband is rarely enough to be happy. Before marriage, having spent time with parents, siblings and friends, you want to continue experiencing those bonds. No matter how loving the partner, you would wish to get a taste of your previous life and not feel too far removed from it. Sati begins to miss her sisters and her mother and wishes to meet her father, with whom she hopes to rekindle the old familiar exhilaration of intellectual discussions.

Soon, an opportunity presents itself. Sati comes to know that her father is organizing a yagya—a large sacrifice in the form of a ceremonial function—since he has been declared a Prajapati. He invites people and creatures from all over the world. There are long descriptions in the Puranas of all those who are invited and who start arriving on different *vahana*s, big and small. Sati watches them and waits for Shiva and herself to get an invitation. As time goes by, it is clear that Daksha has not invited them. Refusing to believe this, an anxious Sati repeatedly pleads with Shiva that they must attend the yagya. Shiva categorically tells her they cannot go. He initially explains kindly why he doesn't deem it correct. He reasons with her and appeals to her good senses that they must not go without an invitation. Slowly, her adamant behaviour makes his annoyance peak and they quarrel. In her heart, Sati is befuddled at her father's exclusion, but to Shiva, she shows a different side. Unyielding, she exclaims, 'I will go and you cannot stop me. I don't need an invite to go to my parents' home.' Ultimately, Sati threatens Shiva, after which Shiva makes his stance clear: No matter what, he would not go. He warns Sati that this act of hers does not augur well and would have dire consequences. Sati is not cowed down by Shiva's warnings and makes the bold move to go by herself.

Sati's stubbornness invokes dread but also love and concern in Shiva. He tries to reason with her, treating her as an absolute equal. There is no ordering her to listen to his command. Instead, he instructs his ganas to accompany her in order to protect her during the long, arduous journey from Mount Kailash to the plains of Haridwar. Each attendant is told by Shiva to carry the things she would need on her journey. His ever-faithful Nandi, who is probably leaving Shiva's side for the first and only time, is to be her vahana; other ganas carry a palanquin, just in case she desires a change from Nandi's back. Another gana holds a parasol to protect her from the sun and rain. Some attendants carry items for her to eat and drink. Shiva has looked after all her comforts for this journey she has embarked upon in a huff. Even as she leaves, confused and tense, she can't help but smile a little at his ministrations. Shiva emerges as an understanding, deeply caring husband who is willing to compromise his own beliefs. He understands when he has to give in and acknowledges that she is an individual and is allowed to exercise her will. In a truly loving relationship, the distinction between oneself and the other is always maintained and preserved. The genuine lover will encourage this separateness and the unique individuality of the beloved.

When Sati reaches her parents' home, she is not welcomed by her father. Instead, Daksha, without hesitation, professes his loathing for Shiva by heaping insult upon insult on him in front of the huge gathering. When Sati asks him why they were not invited, Daksha exclaims in a booming voice, 'Why did you come at all? Your husband is an inauspicious fellow, not conducive to propitiousness. He is ignoble, excluded from the Vedas. He is haughty and evil-minded and of unknown antecedents.' Daksha calls himself a dull-witted sinner since he is the one who gave Sati to Shiva in marriage. He further goes on to tell Sati to abandon the body and be happy.

'All these sutas, asuras, Brahmins and sages bow to me. How is it that this gentleman who is always surrounded by goblins and ghosts behaves like a wicked man? How is it that the shameless frequenter of cremation grounds does not bow to me? Besides, this person is always engrossed in the love of his wife. Hence, I am going to curse him.' Daksha further adds, 'Your husband is known to the wise as inauspicious. He is not of noble lineage. He is the king of goblins, ghosts and spirits of indecent dress and features. Hence, he was not invited.'[11]

At first, being intelligent, Sati tries to reason with her father. She draws out the philosophical aspects of Shiva, but to no avail. Sati is furious and wants to leave her father right away. But where can she go? Should she go back to her abode in the mountains with Shiva? Though she is desirous of seeing him, she does not know what she would say to him. Most importantly, she says that both, he who

85

censures Mahadeva and he who listens when Mahadeva is being censured, go to hell and remain there as long as the moon and the sun shine.[12]

By and by, Daksha's fury spills on to Sati as well and, unable to bear the unending hurling of abuses on her beloved Shiva, she jumps into the sacrificial fire.

When Shiva is informed of this calamitous event by his howling ganas, he pulls at his matted hair in extreme anger and creates Virabhadra, who has a thousand heads, a thousand eyes and a thousand feet; he has a thousand clubs and is clothed in tiger-skin, dripping with blood and bearing a battle axe. With a fierce expression, he rushes to the yagya. Upon reaching there and seeing the catastrophe, he destroys and pollutes the yagya, wreaking all manner of havoc. He then stoops reverentially, lifts the corpse, places it across his shoulders and walks out from the hall, departing with the remains of Sati's body on his shoulder. He begins to dance in a frenzied, wild combination of grief and rage. His grief is naked, his sorrow is raw, on full display for everyone to witness. Blind with agony, babbling to himself like a madman, he wanders across the three worlds in frenzied despair. Seven times, he goes around the world with this burden, majestic in his wrath, and the depth of his grief terrifies the universe. The earth trembles in fear, the soil loses its moisture, the plants die and famine overcomes the land.

Brahma and the other gods observe this and are extremely troubled. They realize that Sati's corpse will not decay as long as it is in contact with Shiva. So, they approach Vishnu for help. With the help of his *sudarshan chakra* (discus), Vishnu dismembers Sati's body and lets the pieces fall to earth. The spots where the pieces fall are considered sites of magical potency. The earth is sacralized at these places which have come in contact with the body of the goddess, thus making her accessible to all her devotees. Sati's death is transformative; through her death she provokes Shiva into direct contact within established religion. Her mythology gives rise to the belief in pilgrimage spots for the worship of the goddess and are called shakti *peeth*s or shakti *sthana*s, literally 'seats' of the goddess. There are fifty-one sites where the limbs of Sati are said to have fallen—Jwalamukhi, Vindhyavasini, Kalighat and Kamakhya are some of the well-known ones. Temples are erected here to the different forms of the devi; the chief object of worship being the goddess.

Shiva challenges conventionally prescribed gender norms and the patriarchal notion of a man having to always appear strong and resolute. Instead, he weeps copiously, wretchedly mourning his dead wife without caring what the world might think. His vulnerability and pathos are on full display. Inconsolable, Shiva begins wandering the earth like a madman and thereby throws the world into a tumult. In some myths, he goes in search of Sati. He eventually finds her in the form of the *yoni* and enters her taking the form of the *linga*, and thus the two remain united forever.

This is the anguish-filled love story of Sati and Shiva. Shiva, content as an ascetic, with absolutely no desire nor intention of entering a marital bond, is eventually drawn into the conjugal fold by Sati. He relishes the married state and is an amorous lover, a protective husband and a wonderful companion before tragedy strikes! This causes him to increase his animosity towards married life and all that it entails. Shiva is a single 'man' again.

The other woman with whom Shiva enters into matrimony is Parvati. In keeping with the Hindu notion of rebirth, Sati returns as Parvati, daughter of Himavat and his wife, Mena, to be his consort the second time around. It must be said here that although Shiva's relationship with the goddess continues to be a dialectical and taut one, she persists in drawing him out of his preferred seclusion and involving him in worldly affairs.

Parvati is a reincarnation of Sati, though her nature is very different. She is a powerful goddess in her own right, and not just Shiva's wife. What she does have in common with Sati is that she takes the lead in pursuing Shiva and eventually succeeds in wooing him with her tapas. Shiva, again truthful to his integral svabhava of being an ascetic, and still smarting from the death of Sati, is most disenchanted and reluctant for another marriage. After many a twist and turn, Shiva and Parvati do get married. Remarkably, Shiva's most important annual festival is Mahashivratri, which is the day of his marriage rather than his day of birth, unlike the celebration of other deities. It is a regular part of the sacred calendar and is celebrated as an elaborate festival in different temple towns of the country, such as Madurai and Khajuraho. So much so that there is even a sculptural type named after their marriage, variously called Kalyanasundaramurti and Parvati Parinaya. During my research, I found many such descriptive sculptures from parts of Madhya Pradesh which portray the wedding ritual of these two great deities. Parvati is usually depicted as the shy bride, with her head bent down. The accompanying gods, Brahma, Vishnu, Narada and Indra, can all be seen participating in the wedding ceremony.

In the Puranas, Parvati and Shiva's relationship appears most beautiful. Let me qualify this—when I say beautiful, I mean that both of them enjoy an intellectual and egalitarian relationship. Sharing, bantering, playing and sporting, all these activities form a vital part of their married life. They indulge in aquatic sports, play on swings, gather flowers, adorn each other, play the lute, paint, draw pictures, discuss the incidents and events of the world and go for rides on Shiva's vahana, Nandi. There are images in stone which depict Parvati facing Shiva with her hand on her chin and expressing rapt concentration, evocative of ongoing conversations between them.

They also indulge in amorous sporting and make love for years on end. We are told they often pass their time with various games, especially favouring the board game Chauser, probably the precursor to modern-day chess. Usually, it is Shiva who wins. Shiva's cronies, known to obsequiously and noisily accompany him mostly everywhere, rejoice and revel by dancing and singing tunelessly. Their buffoonery annoys Parvati no end as they do not even bother to hide where their loyalties lie. Once, Parvati starts winning and tension erupts. Shiva's minions try to salvage the situation by diverting her attention; the ganas accuse her of cheating and lying. This causes her to retaliate by saying that they are partial to Shiva. Narada taunts Parvati, asking who she is trying to win against—is she not aware of the invincibility of Shiva, not just to her but to the entire universe? The pugnacious, faithful Bhringi, at the best of times indifferent to Parvati, now mocks her attempt to defeat his omnipotent lord. He plays all his cards to rattle her. She looks up sharply as he recounts Shiva's effortless burning of Kama and wanton decapitating of Daksha and the contamination of his prestigious sacrifice. Parvati curses Bhringi for always butting in between the two and says he would have to live without an inch of flesh on his body—in other words, as a bag of bones. So often, this faithful follower of Shiva is seen in sculpture with his rib cage exposed and three thin, reed-like legs supporting him, barely able to stand. The same curse is directed at him in another episode where the Ardhanarishvara image originates, and a helplessly fleshless, bent, bony Bhringi is to be seen in sculpture, hobbling along on three legs, the extra leg provided by the ever-compassionate Shiva.

Eventually, as victory is imminent, a triumphant and playful Parvati, after every move, asks Shiva to take off one of his valued possessions, which she keeps as her prize. She asks for the crescent moon and seizes it, annulates it and wears it as an earring. Then she asks for the serpent, Vasuki, which adorns Shiva's neck. One by one, she takes possession of all his scant attire and ornaments. Lastly, she asks for his loin cloth. In the stunned silence that ensues, Shiva's troops avert their faces in modesty. A hitherto quiet and now flabbergasted Shiva asks her what kind of wife commands her husband to become nude in front of a gathering.

Parvati reminds him of his ascetic, wild days when he would roam naked and aroused in front of all the sages' wives in the Daruvana forest. 'What do you have to do with a loin cloth, you hermit? You are a sanctified soul. Some time back, you wandered through Daruvana with the cardinal points alone for your garments. You have no sense of shame!' Parvati taunts Shiva, possibly taking revenge for her past humiliation. After an uncomfortable pause, Parvati relents and allows Shiva to keep his loin cloth.

When I recounted this story at my lectures in America, audiences would initially be astonished before their hesitant giggles turned into open laughter. Eventually, they applauded and suggested that Shiva and Parvati seemed to be playing strip poker! It amused them a great deal to see a heavenly couple breaking away from the conventional roles of man and wife, especially in the Indian context. What I find remarkable is the depiction of a wife chastening her husband in a public arena and getting away with it, sans any dire and hideous consequences. Here is a couple in the godly world which breaks from conformist norms and creates a unique relationship with harmless banter.

Shiva also gives in to Parvati's desire to be half of his body, and thus we see the composite hybrid image, Ardhanarishvara. Parvati's body is his and his body is hers. There are some amusing and charming stories of Parvati's jealous rage at Ganga, another beautiful woman seated on Shiva's head forever, and Parvati's fear of her flowing and making her way through his ear to his very heart. This wrangle, though in itself a very colourful one, brings out Shiva's generous and self-assured nature. He plays fair and 'allows' Parvati to have heated discussions with him, reason with him and even sometimes dominate him. What is pleasantly surprising is the fact that Shiva can handle such a strong, almost insouciant wife. In fact, Shiva is the only god who has an outspoken wife and perhaps the only deity who does not try to be dominant. Only a self-confident male can coexist with such a female. I may be faulted for using a modern concept, but to me it appears to be a democratic relationship. It exemplifies understanding, reconciliation, mutual respect and, of course, love.

We are constantly told that the struggle against *ahamkara*—egoism—is the hardest battle a human being has to fight. The 'ego dwarf' has a nasty habit of seeing everything exclusively in relation to itself and projecting itself on all other things, distorting and discolouring them.

Because of its fluid reality, it entangles itself increasingly in error, loneliness and fear. Metaphorically, Shiva is the destroyer of the ego. Through his meditation, he destroys the ego within himself. We should know when we need to let go of our ego, and when to give it rein. It's all about staying calm. The process may begin when we are young and eventually it should become part of our personality. It is also said that the ego needs to be submerged. This whole sense of I, me, mine or *mamatva* ('I-ness') needs to dissolve. It should not always be about you. The scriptures ask us to be expansive human beings. More than submerging or destroying the ego, we should learn how to manage it. Why do we have egos that just can't accept defeat? We should try to assimilate the belief that giving in to someone you love is not defeat. This is a powerful way to manage the ego. Shiva gives in and admits defeat even when it is in a game.

Isn't it but natural for conflicts to arise between two people living in close proximity? In a relationship, it is usually the woman who bears the brunt of her male partner's anger and temper. Sadly enough, we find that those marriages have just about lasted the course where one half of a couple is reticent and lets the other hold centre stage. Shiva and Parvati's situation is so much better. Neither is daunted by the other. Secondly, no matter how tough confrontations are—whether it is through dialogue, fighting, tears or arguments—anything is better than silence. This is amply demonstrated by Shiva and Parvati.

Loving spouses can repeatedly challenge each other if the marital relationship is to serve the function of promoting the mental growth of partners. Shiva and Parvati certainly don't believe in the silent treatment that many couples have been guilty of from times immemorial. If something troubles them, they address it right away.

Silence harms a relationship as it eclipses the purpose of the anger in the first place. When couples push all differences under the proverbial carpet, it is a form of emotional cutting-off which, in the long run, can extinguish a bond. Even if it makes one feel temporarily in control, it leads to an emotional deadlock, because by shutting off, one is withdrawing from any scope to understand the issue. I know of couples who foster and germinate a false harmony between themselves by never appearing to disagree.

I questioned those whose marriages had been annulled or had come to the brink of divorce, and others who were even worse off as they just stayed together, unable to even be civil with each other. The couples confessed that in the past and even now, when any major issue came up between them, they would push it under the connubial bed. The reason for the tension could be anything—from the most banal to the most tragic. There were the usual reasons: unwanted house guests, in-laws' demands, disproportionate preference of one set of parents, kids performing badly at school, either partner paying excessive attention to someone of the opposite sex. These situations led to resentful silences and the breakdown of communication. Some reasons are far darker and the issue far more permanent—the death of a child, a major disease or the onset of disability, to mention a few. Silence is a fallout of the inability to deal with sudden and tragic changes, among other things. Couples claimed they would not confront each other as their sleeping children would get disturbed at raised voices, or they had an early morning day of work to dash off to, or even worse, they did not see the dire nature of what they were conniving in, or the spouse was incapable of any understanding—all piecemeal excuses that contributed to tearing them apart in the long run. Both partners turn their backs on the gnawing suspicions, lurking doubts and disappointments, till the silence develops into full-blown calcified hatred and the point of no return.

It is better to send the kids off to play, shut the bedroom door, sit down and be honest and upfront and look for solutions. It's okay to shout, cry, apologize and confess, and hopefully have the next fight over something new, and not on the same issue. Remove from the admiration lists the men you know who stayed quiet when their wives yelled and were totally unreasonable, or those women who were such doting, faithful wives that they tolerated all kinds of nonsense from their husbands without uttering a word. Then compare them to the couple which was ready to have discussions, speak up and have room for disagreement, and not shy away from speaking honestly.

Shiva and Parvati's lovemaking, suffused with amorous banter, is a topic of strife now and then. It is said that the artful Parvati curves and whirls around the stock-still Shiva, just like the vine or creeper winds its way upwards around a tree. Many such images may have come directly from observing nature or they may have been prompted by artistic considerations. In the Padma Purana, it is stated that at one such time Shiva is gloating over his 'white body' (Shiva looks 'white' with ashes covering his body) and teasing Parvati, who looks 'Kali' in comparison and remarks, 'Joined with him, her body would shine like a black female serpent clung to a white sandalwood tree.'[13] Parvati is irked by what she considers an insult and angrily retorts that neither is she crooked like a serpent or rough, instead, Shiva is known to the world as possessing poison and as being a shelter to the 'mines of faults [those who commit faults]'. She goes on to make references to other myths and tells him that he is the one who snatched away the teeth of Pushan and destroyed Bhaga's eyes. He cannot afford to call her black as he himself is known as Mahakala.

There is no sign of an eager-to-pacify Parvati rushing off to do tapas in order to remove the dark sheath and become Gauri, the fair-complexioned one, 'to please her lord'. But she is opinionated and wary of Shiva's attributes and his past doings, which she reminds him of when she refers to Bhaga and Pushan. She wants to leave in order to abandon herself by means of penance as she had been insulted by a 'rogue' and he created 'a headache in her'.

In one more occurrence in the Skanda Purana, Shiva tells Parvati that she is behaving like her father, and her mind is overpowered with turbidness, like the mass of clouds on the peak of the Himalayan mountains. She had taken hardness from the stones, thickness from the thickets, crookedness from the rivers and made herself difficult to be employed, like the snow. All these traits, Shiva tells Parvati, have been transferred to her by her father.[14] Parvati replies, 'From serpents you have received many tongues, from the ashes you have got oiliness, and the wickedness in your heart has sprung from the moon. You have no sense of shame because you are naked.'[15]

In the Vayu Purana, Parvati curses Agni and calls him evil-minded for interrupting their lovemaking before she has been satisfied. She is such a strong voice that she tells Agni that he will forever carry black smoke about him and appear like a man disfigured by leprosy.

Many people wonder why young girls want husbands like Shiva. I feel this could be because Shiva is very real with his imperfections and in his antics very colourful. Most importantly, he has an equal and loving relationship with his wife which exemplifies playfulness, mild sparring, understanding, reconciliation and mutual respect. Both take centre stage in the drama of their world.

The relationship between Shiva and his wife appears to be a non-hierarchical one. Seen through the lens of the patriarchal set-up in times of yore, it is truly astounding and unique. In this context, it is interesting to compare them to another divine duo, Lakshmi and Vishnu. Lakshmi is familiar to everyone and is worshipped daily in households and offices. Additionally, she is the beautiful goddess who pays homes a 'visit' during the festival of Diwali. Remarkably, in these prominent areas of religiosity, there's no mention or pre-eminent position given to her spouse, Vishnu. Furthermore, in texts like the Puranas, rarely do we hear of any chatter and natter between the two. It won't be an exaggeration to say that the association sometimes even gets forgotten. The same applies to other divine twosomes. In the plastic arts, Lakshmi is very often depicted massaging Vishnu's feet. She is also a victim of the iconographic method to indicate hierarchy where she is shown anatomically very small in size as compared to Vishnu.

When this representation is compared to that of Shiva and Parvati, we realize that the latter is the only couple in Indian mythology which has an equality of status between the husband and the wife. The bond which Shiva has with his wives is very rare. His relationships with Sati and then with Parvati are on an equal footing wherein Shiva does not assert his superiority. Rather, he accepts his spouse to be an intellectual companion. This understanding makes for an ideal couple. Even though they may appear imperfect in their dealings with each other, with all the disagreeing and tussling and fussing, theirs is actually a relationship based on negotiation and dialogue. Through Shiva's attitude towards his wives, we can see him managing his ego. He is the great yogi, the great knower, and although he knows how to play supreme lord and master to an adoring Parvati, he also knows how to give in when she is his spouse and submit totally to her in her form as Devi.

In another episode in the life of Shiva and Parvati, Shiva, in his ignorance, ego and anger, beheads Ganesha. When Parvati comes to know, she is beside herself with grief. She implores Shiva to breathe life into him once again. Shiva does not argue or hesitate. He realizes his mistake and plants the head of the first living being he encounters—an elephant—onto the boy's torso, and that is how Ganesha gets his elephant head. This is another example of Shiva giving in to his wife's requests. He tries to understand and reconcile and ultimately arrive at a solution to respect her. Similarly, we should have the courage to speak up on the first sign of trouble; don't wait for it to reach a stage of murkiness. The little unattended resentments grow over time, like barnacles. Do not procrastinate; the sooner you address an issue, the faster you can work it out. Here, I would like to mention something I have learnt through several interviews and experience. It is astonishing for me to see continued physical and sexual intimacy in marriages that are sorely lacking in communication. There is a cliché that 'make-up sex' after a massive fight is wonderful. Clearly, the couples in question are deluding themselves by the false impression that things are fine between them. They are probably convinced that the rhythm of physical intimacy will shield them from future hurt. But this is not sufficient and does not help in fostering love, respect or a comprehensive understanding of the source of the tension. What matters most, then, is talking, communicating and listening. Human lives are shaped by both subjective and objective truths. One should attempt to move away from *vivaad*, that is, argument, where we only seek to prove the other wrong, to *samvaad*, discussion, where we get to know of the other's opinions and learn to respect each other, as exemplified by Shiva and Parvati.

There is a glory in love when a couple stays together after successfully ironing out their issues. It isn't going to be a smooth journey, and reaching the 'companion phase' is an uphill climb, when you can celebrate your offspring's lives and spend time with grandchildren, or travel together and be content with the gentler rhythms of life in your late fifties and sixties.

A long-term relationship goes through many phases; there may be times of suspicion, restlessness, boredom, ennui and several other feelings. The quality and tenor of love with the same person, year after year, has to change and accommodate the mutations that take place over time. Admittedly, with the passage of time, your partner may seem like a completely different person from when you initially relished them in the first flush of love. As the years go by, love should arouse different feelings, different expectations. The notion of romance should change.

One can develop a pattern, an idea of love that leaves no room for passion, if passion is defined as shouting, fighting or communicating in what appears to be an intense way. There can be a desire to extend acceptance and autonomy, a sort of independent dependence in the relationship, as the years go by. Then you can witness the satisfaction of endurance and the cosiness of abundant memories of a shared life, whether it is taking pride in building a home together, living vicariously through well-settled children or maintaining close bonds with friends and relatives. The kind of ardour one begins a relationship with changes as the years progress. One should not continue expecting the same behaviour from a spouse; it will be replaced with a different type of intimacy which comes with the familiarity of knowing each other over so many years. The surprise of sexual romance may fade away, and to know that it's okay is a relief. In fact, those who consider sex the only focus in a relationship have a difficult time as they grew older. If the media and self-help books are to be believed, sex is said to be the key to a great relationship, but if one solely follows this dictum, it may lead to a lack of investment of time, effort and heartache in transforming a relationship from the physical to the emotional.

There can be many reasons for a rift in a couple's life. In the godly terrain, the power between Shiva and Parvati is clearly divided. She, a commanding goddess, has her followers and he has his. Yet, they come together in a mutually dependent independent way. In the human world, this 'power' can be translated as the financial aspect of a relationship. A key factor that makes for a well-adjusted couple is financial independence. A large portion of life is easier and tension-free if the money flow is adequate. But there should not be just one person taking care of the finances as that can be an unfair burden.

Do not put all your eggs in one basket. Have your own independent relationships other than the one you share with your partner. Shiva is known to go off with his cronies and partake of a relaxing hallucinogen, and indulge in 'alone time' and meditation. Parvati has her friends, Jaya and Vijaya, who help her in her ablutions and other aspects of life. They both also have their own 'portfolios' in the celestial world and keep very busy, away from each other. They give each other, as they say in today's times, 'space'. We should have people other than our spouses in our lives to enrich it and to be there when we need a sounding board or advice—siblings, cousins, friends, colleagues or neighbours. Let bonhomie and understanding come from many directions! Additionally, your relationships with different people make you an interesting person to be around.

Beginning an intimate relationship with another person is always a risk. It comes with a sense of vulnerability, which can dissolve the cognitive space with which we surround and protect ourselves. The risk of rejection, the fear of dependence, etc. are all part of being close to one person. Eventually, we have to make our choices on how we prefer to live life.

In the Shiva narrative, there are long-standing debates between two seemingly incompatible life orientations:

that of the ascetic and that of the married person. As these are played out through various media—sculpture, myth, ritual and popular culture—it seems that the world of Shiva offers reasonable arguments in favour of a domestic conjugal life.

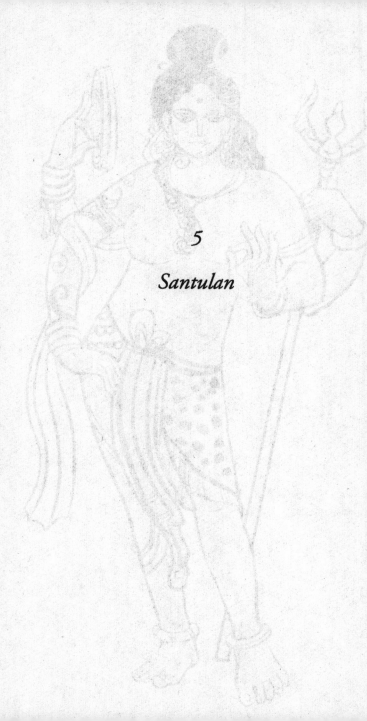

5

Santulan

> *There are afflictions of the body*
> *There are fluctuations of the mind*
> *Bring in a life of balance*
> *Leave them all behind.*

There are about forty-five words for 'balance' in Sanskrit, which is indicative of its importance in this age-old culture. These include *samatvam*, *samadhama*, *samyam*, *samayayuktah* and *samata*, to mention a few. Their meanings have specific nuances but they are basically all similar and can be translated as perfect restraint, mental balance and equanimity. For the concepts of equilibrium, evenness, symmetry and equipoise being examined in this chapter, I prefer the idea of two words put together: sama and *tula*, which mean equal and balance respectively. Once you have balance, you will have composure, aplomb and sangfroid. *Santulan* is a stage that each and everybody should aspire for. It is nigh impossible to maintain it throughout one's life. Even the most composed person, at some point or the other, has lost his or her balance.

The word 'balance' is bandied about a lot these days. In current parlance, it is understood in mainly two ways. Firstly, in the sense of striking a balance between work and play or between home and office. Secondly, in the sense that everything should be done in a balanced way, be it eating, drinking, sleeping, partying, loving, caring or hating. In the venerable realm of the gods, the opposite of balance is chaos. During different cosmic cycles, whenever there is a sense of imbalance in the Indic world, avatars have descended to restore it. The sense of balance seems to have been of great importance to the ancient mind.

The very nature of balance is such that it is something towards which we have to work; it does not come about naturally. All children have to be taught balance—in other words, the rules and discipline of living. You can't play all day; you have to sleep at a proper time; you have to bathe; you have to eat—these are some of the lessons ingrained into us as children. Even as we grow into young adults, we have to consciously apply the principle of balance to our lives as we can go off kilter very easily. There won't be a single person who has not gobbled up a jumbo pack of banana chips or potato wafers or some other delectable snack of little nutritious value, or had to suffer the consequences of a night of uncontainable revelry. Then there are those people who keep blabbering about their achievements or those who continually whinge about their bosses as long-suffering listeners roll their eyes. Excess can be seen everywhere.

To be balanced is to not be addicted to anything or anyone. Therefore, when we lose all sense of equilibrium, we seek therapy. We may be eating too much, wanting too much sex, being too possessive of someone or shopping till we are broke—we can do with balance at all these times. Some of us have a natural tilt towards an extreme nature and believe it is all or nothing, always. If we fall into this category, then the earlier we become aware of this debilitating characteristic, the longer we will have to rectify it or at least modify it. Living with it unattended can prove to be quite disastrous.

In a rather unique manner, Shiva epitomizes balance in his life choices, because not only is he Mahayogi, an ascetic, he is also Shankara, the beneficent married one. He balances two opposites. How this paradox is understood by his devotees is that he is inherently an ascetic, but because of the requests of the world and his own desire to help, he marries and becomes a householder. Otherwise, as just a renunciate, Shiva would not be concerned or even aware of the various issues of the world and would not have the experience of procreation. He would not be able to empathize with the ups and downs and the tribulations of married life. So, ultimately, Shiva succumbs to the demands of the time and has the rare distinction of being an ascetic and the only deity in the Hindu pantheon to have a full-fledged family.

In his persona, in his mythology, in his very being, Shiva straddles opposites, rendering him as enigmatic, ambiguous and entertaining. I believe it is not enough to listen to the stories; we can actually look at him for life lessons, that is, if we can see through the maze of contradictions. He is a householder—a loved and cherished husband and a much-admired father. Shiva does not abstain from the pleasures of the body or from the bliss of family. He is *sarvabhogin*, that is, one who enjoys all pleasures. Yet, when the need arises, he removes himself from the lived world and escapes to his inner world, to seek refurbishment and answers to troubling situations inside as well as outside him.

So how can Shiva be an ascetic if he enjoys all worldly pleasures? His asceticism lies in his ability to control and regulate his mind and emotions. From time to time, Shiva detaches himself and adopts a practically alternative lifestyle that epitomizes introspection and makes him appear restrained and dispassionate. In mythical episodes, we can witness this in his encounters with other deities. He does not get into petty fights with Brahma, Vishnu or others over matters such as who is the greatest among them all. Instead, he comes to the rescue when there is complete chaos and disorder. He stabilizes the world because he has that power of mind which enables him to have the best of both worlds, materially and spiritually.

There is a Shaivic myth which conveys, in a very poignant manner, the importance of balance. Once Sati burns herself to death in the sacrificial fire, the grief-stricken Shiva's mourning takes gargantuan form. Like a demented person, he carries the dead Sati on his shoulder and dances the dreadful, macabre dance of anguish. The entire earth gets into a frenzy along with him, causing cosmic imbalance and almost bringing the world to a dystopian end. Everything comes to a standstill. But balance has to be restored and it eventually is.

If we apply this to real life, we can understand why we should not hold on to a corpse. The final rites have to be performed and the corporal body has to be disposed of. The reality of loss has to be accepted. Step by step, death has to be dealt with, and after the required time has lapsed, an attempt to restore normalcy has to be made.

In the myth of Sati's death, the entire celestial world is also shaken up, and none of the gods have the courage to approach Shiva to commiserate, to soothe him or point out the futility of it all. In total despair and helplessness, fearing for their own future, the gods seek the help of Vishnu, at times a rival of Shiva who is often made to look small in comparison to Shiva's loftiness. He comes into this scenario as a saviour and a worried comrade. In order to stop the relentless frenzy which has continued unabated for so long, Vishnu dismembers the body of Sati with his weapon, the chakra (discus), until nothing is left. One by one, the beautiful Sati's body parts—breasts, ears, eyes, the vagina—fall from the skies, and the places where they came to rest throughout the subcontinent become spots of potency. Today, the different sites are considered the pithas or seats of the goddess. Tied up in a sacred geography, giving a raison d'etre for her shrines, they became forceful places of worship. Thereby, Vishnu brings an end to the mayhem and also makes Shiva accept that his wife is dead. The heartbroken Shiva retreats to the mountains. In some myths, he goes in search of Sati, eventually finding her in the form of the yoni. He takes the form of the linga and enters her, and thus the two remain united forever. Essentially, Shiva has to relearn how to live in a balanced way after the tragedy unhinges his blissful life.

Like most societies, the Hindu world is prone to excess. To redress this issue, the Brahminical mind had put forth a template. The social structure, the caste system, the Purusharthas—artha, dharma, kama, moksha, varnashramadharma—were all created to bring about a balance in society. Certainly, this 'balance' in the past was to favour a certain section of society, and was unpardonably hierarchical and exploitative. In addition, we are not sure if it was always followed, but the rules were definitely put in place theoretically. There is the *chaturvarna*, the caste system, for balance in society, and then there are the four ashramas for balance in an individual's lifespan.

Despite the injunctions, there are, now and then, signs of society sidestepping the set norms. For example, at one time, many young people were renouncing the prescribed, ordered way of life and becoming wandering mendicants, pursuing an alternative lifestyle. These people were not necessarily interested in carrying out Brahminical life rituals or samskaras. In the ordered way of life, samskaras such as the marriage ritual or the naming ceremony were considered essential, and, more importantly, the avenue from where priests would receive their dana and dakshina, that is, their livelihood. The wanderers did not marry or have offspring or light the daily hearth. To offset this situation, the four ashramas were introduced. The laws of Manu and, subsequently, most of Hindu philosophy, divide the upper-caste male's life into four broad ashramas—that is, stages or phases of life—with unique objectives. It is made abundantly clear that one can change goals only once one passes to the next ashrama. This way, an attempt at a state of equilibrium, albeit by diktat, is secured. Like many things within Hinduism, the concept of individual freedom exists but with a rider—you can renounce the ordered life of a householder, but at the 'right' time, that is, when you are of a mature age, when no samskara is left to be performed, except for death itself.

The *brahmacharya* phase is from ages twelve to twenty. In this period, the male youngster is a student and he has to stay with his guru or mentor. His primary duty is hence, towards his guru and the study of the Vedas. His main goals are education, celibacy and self-discipline. In the *grihstha* phase, he is a householder, which entails marriage, children and economic well-being. As the *yajamana* or the patriarch, he is to perform yagyas and be the patron bestowing dana or alms to Brahmins and the needy.

In *vanaparathstha*, the yajamana is now at least fifty years old and transmutes to become the dweller in the woods. He has performed all his duties and now retired to a quiet life. He can fill his day with religious meditation, with all responsibilities handed over to the next generation. He is to prepare for ultimate death through contemplation and focusing on spiritual thoughts.

Sannyasa is the last ashrama, where the individual has reached the stage of being a mendicant, free to roam about and beg for alms. This is a period of complete renunciation and one that concentrates on detachment, reducing desires to the bare minimum and seeking moksha. The ashrama system epitomizes the saying that there is a time and place for everything. It is not always strictly adhered to but the template exists. It also shows the crucial nature of balance that we require and the path which, once theoretically provided, may be emulated.

In essence, an individual's life, if it is keyed to the idea of balance—of thought, perspective, attitude, attributes, behaviour and conduct—can lead to a serene existence. Balance, in various aspects of life, is conducive to good health and longevity. If 'indulgences' are partaken of in a balanced way, on certain occasions only, there will always be something to look forward to.

Buddhism also advocates the Middle Path or the path of moderation. It exhorts one to avoid extremes. Following this path ensures happiness for oneself and others, yielding the greatest value to human existence. Moderation is the key to an ideal life, even in our day-to-day, mundane activities like eating, sleeping and recreation, the pursuit of wealth, acquisition of knowledge, seeking of life goals—everything needs to be tempered and requires a balance to yield the desired results. Even virtues, if not exercised in the right proportion, lose their sublimity.

Perfectionism has long been an admired trait, with people exalting it as the finest quality. In fact, some suffer from a pathology of perfection, so much so that they cease to distinguish between those chores that just need to get done and those which will profit when an attempt at perfection is made. Perfection is a highly overrated virtue which can keep you much busier than you need to be and make you neurotic with the expectations it creates. I have observed the unhappiness it has caused those who strive for it and those who have to live with a perfectionist. For instance, I feel sorry for people who keep impeccable homes but have no visitors. They make guests feel acutely uncomfortable with their constant watching out for spills, dirty footwear and playful children scrambling over sofas. Since perfectionism is an inherent trait of mine, I had to work on myself. It was difficult to completely eliminate it, and I also realized it could be a big advantage if practised in moderation. I compromised and consciously sought perfection in only those areas of my life which are in my control, and, more importantly, which give me lifelong satisfaction.

All kind-hearted people are moved by others' misfortunes. But even here, a balance should be maintained and we should not let the unhappiness and miseries of others' lives accumulate within us. We must try to help someone in trouble and express sympathy but not keep looking out for unhappy people and getting worked up. We should endeavour to rise above both happiness and sorrow, whether they are our own or somebody else's. We shouldn't allow emotions to clutter our minds. Charity should also be done within sensible proportions. Some people don't know where to draw boundaries, and work tirelessly for others, neglecting their own homes and families. Others will rush to help and then acquire a veritable halo, sermonizing with egregious holier-than-thou attitudes.

Imbalances and extremities are encountered all the time. When we think of extremities at a practical level, we realize that they actually hinder our life cycle. We all need to bring about a balance, or *sayyam*, in our lives. Even if some people are not completely balanced in the ways described above, they know the importance of staying calm and in control of one's mind and actions. The most admired human beings are the ones who are in control of their senses. That is actually what we all need to strive for. A central idea found as early as in the Rig Veda is *rta*, which means harmony or order. The word for seasons, *ritu*, comes from this Sanskrit word. It means the observance of natural phenomena, of the sun and moon, day and night, and the seasons. It was clear to the earliest humans that their days and seasons followed a pattern, that nature could be benevolent and beautiful yet malevolent and menacing.

When we talk about extremities, we are often faced with various, mostly negative, reactions. The extreme side of human nature has been celebrated in painting, music and many other highly revered art forms. Some people feel that it is actually only the intense moments of truth which bring out the best paintings, the most heart-rending music, and the finest poetry. The folly of love—an extreme emotion—is what makes for a riveting romance. I have memories of being a teenager and glancing out of the window to find a lovelorn youth standing in pouring rain, waiting to get a glimpse of me, and of another time when an admirer stood in the corridors of his school dormitory as my school bus passed so he could get a fleeting glimpse, provided I had managed a window seat. Very often, his lunch break would end and he would have to starve till dinnertime. It probably made him feel ever more the heroic Romeo. Today, we can dismiss such behaviour as a waste of time and energy.

Remarkably and ironically, extremes are what we like to see portrayed on screen. Look at the steady popularity of the Devdas theme—how many times will the same movie be made for different generations? Yet, each rendition is almost always a commercial success. Is it because we feel all the rasa when we watch a protagonist who has no sense of balance allow his life to become full of despondent despair? It should be enough to watch such stories on screen or read of such lives in fiction. In our own lives, it is a stolid and stable mien that comforts and that we yearn for. When we are young, we might recover from a long-drawn-out fight with a spouse or a sibling. But if we have to do the same at an advanced age, it is depleting and depressing. So, in our thirties and forties we should strive for an almost boring equilibrium. When I look back at the recklessness and frenzied lifestyle that took a toll on some people I knew, I feel some of us are lucky to have escaped with minimum damage. Others have died young, or worse, become incapacitated. Balance is vital, not just for the old fogeys but for everyone at all stages of life.

It is said that you can never have enough of a good thing. This is not true. Even an overdose of the 'good things' can cause anxiety. Some of us, for instance, are made uncomfortable by extreme generosity; it has a suffocating effect and makes the receiver feel inadequate compared with the giver.

Love is a prerequisite for all personal relationships, but an excess of it can likewise wreak havoc. It is also often misplaced. For example, it may get transmuted into possessiveness, creating misery, and in extreme cases lead to the horror of stalking.

I knew of an elderly man who loved his wife so much that he never wanted their children to complain to her about the most mundane things. If the food was not tasty, for example, they were never to say a word. They suppressed whatever was bothering them throughout the time they lived under their parents' roof. When they eventually developed anxiety and had to go to therapists, it naturally entailed childhood issues getting examined. The mother was astonished and hurt and felt betrayed, crying and telling them that if they had pointed these things out to her earlier, she would have done things differently. I'm not sure the father's protective love towards his wife, the mother of his children, was beneficial to anyone.

Parenthood can bring out the best in some individuals. They become protective, sacrificing and playful, realizing, with some surprise, that it is possible to care far more for someone else than for themselves. But when it comes to parenting, one should be cautious not to lose all sense of 'self'. For example, take a mother's love for her daughter. What happens when a mother gives endlessly, to the point of drowning her own interests, hobbies, ambitions; all her time dedicated to the daughter? Sometimes, realization dawns too late, by which time behavioural patterns have been formed. A mother should be able to strike a balance and not indulge each and every desire of her child. The latitude a child enjoys should be balanced. All anxiously doting mothers should be aware that children grow to admire mothers who are able to strike a balance. Children should be brought up with the knowledge that they are not the only pivot of their mother's lives and that they have other interests as well. Believing this makes children less egoistic and more compassionate.

Even desires should be balanced. We should not crave for things totally beyond our reach. Stalking somebody or constantly hankering after them, needless to say, is dangerous. I would like to be able to partake of the finer things in life—such as a glass of wine or any other alcohol, or rich food—throughout my life, and in order to do so, I have to consume them in a balanced manner. Anything in moderation is usually not harmful. I will hopefully not be told to stop consuming the things I like due to some ailment or the other. A famous Indian author lived to be a hundred, and because he balanced his intake of liquor, he never had to put a complete stop to something he enjoyed. Balance always helps in the long run. In order to enjoy something for a longer period, one has to learn how to not go overboard. I know quite a few people—now in their fifties—with successful careers and fulfilling personal lives who occasionally smoke marijuana. It is their way of relaxing and dealing with life's stresses. There are also discussions worldwide about it actually being better for health than alcohol.

We need to balance not just our emotions but most things in life. For instance, we should not focus excessively on work. Some people work so hard that they lose sight of other goals; they get obsessed. Even though they succeed professionally, they ignore the lighter side of life and constantly talk just about their work, taking themselves very seriously.

It would be useful to set boundaries for ourselves. How much should we work? How much weight should we lose? Many jobs and careers are inherently designed to ensure you have no boundaries. I know of someone who worked in a Japanese multinational company where leaving at 6 p.m. (the official timing) was frowned upon and looked at as dereliction of duty. The poor man never reached home on time; he ruined his relationship with his young wife, who walked out on him, and his children hardly remember having their father around. Working hard in short bursts is fine, but for such a pace to go on with no end in sight is fraught.

We also have to look after our health in a balanced way. Some of us pore over articles on the internet and search for symptoms, driving both well-wishers and doctors up the wall. Some of us talk about ailments in graphic detail even in reply to a polite random enquiry, such as 'How are you?' while the enquirer, swamped with details they could have done without, is making a mental note to never ask again. When do we know that we are going over the top? We can check the situation by being alert to the listener's reaction. This will make us pause when we see we have lost their attention, and we can then ask them about their lives.

Some of us are always waiting for the perfect time to carry out a particular activity or use a particularly coveted thing we own. That perfect time is never in the present but always in the future. It rarely arrives, and items to be used by a certain date get ruined and have to be thrown away unused. Such people take hoarding to the extreme: 'I will use these coloured drinking glasses only when somebody special visits, I will use this expensive bug spray on an important guest, I will take out the embroidered hand towels when we have house guests—let's make do with scraps of old clothes in the meantime.' In some cases, children who were longing to partake of the item have moved out of the house. Ask the offspring who has to go to her deceased mother's home to find all the things she hoarded, which are now in an unusable state. Her mother never enjoyed them and neither did any member of her family. She had no balanced idea of what and how much to save for a rainy day and how to enjoy the moment in front of her. When this lady passed away and her daughter went to the house to relinquish the keys to the landlord, she couldn't stop crying. She saw all the unused items, so many of them rotting away and of no use to anyone. She saw the neighbours trying to hide their sniggers at the things that were disembowelled from the small, cramped house. There is so much regret that comes with imbalance in such an instance. We all must learn how to live in the moment.

There is the balance of the world that Shiva restores. There is his own mental and physical balance. But the most remarkable example of balance can be seen in the noteworthy composite image of Shiva as Ardhanarishvara, an epithet that is translated as 'the lord who is half woman'. Perhaps a more accurate description is half male, half female. In this image, Shiva is seen balancing within his being both his own and his spouse's body. He is the first god to have such a two-in-one form, though the conceptual roots can be seen in the idea of dual deities, prevalent as far back as the time of the Rig Veda: Agni–Soma, Mitra–Varuna and Dyava–Prithvi. A reworking of this dual-deity motif is found in the prakriti–purusha concept of Samkhya philosophy. The right half is that of Shiva, whose hands show a gesture of fearlessness, holding the *pasha* (noose), along with the jatamukuṭa. Garments made of tiger skin cover the body from the waist to the knees. In some north Indian representations, the half-*urdhvareta* (ithyphallic) feature is visible on the right male side. The left side shows Parvati's locks elegantly arranged in the traditional ornamented hairstyle called *dhamilla*; she is also wearing earrings and a headdress or *karanda mukuta*. A well-rounded female breast distinguishes the torso on the left female side. The straighter line of Shiva's body contrasts with a curvaceous waist and rounded hip. Other female emblems include a *nilotpala* (blue lotus) and *darpaṇa* (mirror).

These aspects of Ardhanarishvara have attracted scholars to look at the image primarily as an example of dual or composite iconographic representation. There is no classical myth for this imagery and therefore it is interpreted in a number of ways, including one where Shiva is said to have generated Parvati from his own substance in the formless void that preceded creation. Shiva and Parvati melt into each other and become Ardhanarishvara in a fusion of matter and consciousness.

In the fifth century, the poet Kalidasa originally expanded on the concept of Ardhanarishvara. In the beginning of *Raghuvamsha*, there is a verse dedicated to Shiva and Parvati. Kalidasa says the two have a harmonious union, inextricably conjoined, just like a word. The *artha* of the word—that is, the meaning—is masculine. And the *vak*—that is, the diction—is feminine. The idea that a strong couple is one that retains the individual identity of each half strongly suggests that Kalidasa was familiar with Ardhanarishvara temple icons as popular objects of worship. He referred to the god and goddess with one dual compound term and described the image with the adjective 'whose left half is his wife'—*vamardhajani*. This image represents the unification of an ostensibly dualistic divinity, the ultimate non-duality of Shiva and Shakti.

When we think of extremities at a practical, everyday level, we realize that they essentially hinder our progress. Hindu prayers end with the invocation of 'shanti'. It seems the ancient Hindu mind knew the importance of staying calm and in control of our mind and actions. The most admired human being is one who is in control of his or her senses. That is actually what we all need to strive for.

Another imbalance that affects us on a day-to-day basis and makes us miserable is oversensitivity. Some people claim with pride that they are so. One suggestion is to minimize the circle of people who can make you overwrought. Not everyone should be allowed to hold that favoured position so effortlessly. What worked for me when I was young and oversensitive and brooding all the time over this and that was to realize that the person who hurt me has moved on. I was only making myself miserable while the other person was probably not even thinking about me any more or imagining what they said or did had had such a dire effect.

Shiva is composed of two opposite beings: the archetypal ascetic who regularly does tapas and also someone who has a family. He basically reconciles two extremes within his own personality. Actually, why just two, there are many sides to Shiva. The peacefulness of a meditating mind, the anger at being disturbed, the heightened love for Sati, the tragic display of mourning at her demise, the playfulness with Parvati, and being the silent teacher with Brahma and Vishnu—these are all facets of his personality. He is quiescent, he is volatile, he is steady as a dancer and as a slayer, and he is fair as a father. These are the multiple manifestations. Is it not the same in our lives? We can benefit by dipping into all the juices, so to say. We have much to glean from delving deep within ourselves, but it is also easy to get lost in the web of the inner life. Sure, the unexamined life is not worth living, but if all you are doing is examining your life then that is not worthwhile either. Self-examination must not render us introverts. It must not undermine the worth of our engagements with others, for companionship, for learning from their experiences and for taking assistance when needed. Then again, it is easy to get lost in the jingle-jangle of the crowd. Life should be spent like a wheel, so that we enjoy solitude and then the company of people and then only one person—alternating one after the other. We should have the dexterity to use what we learn in one mode as a check and balance to the other. Shiva brings about a balance, inviting all the forces in his life, in his world.

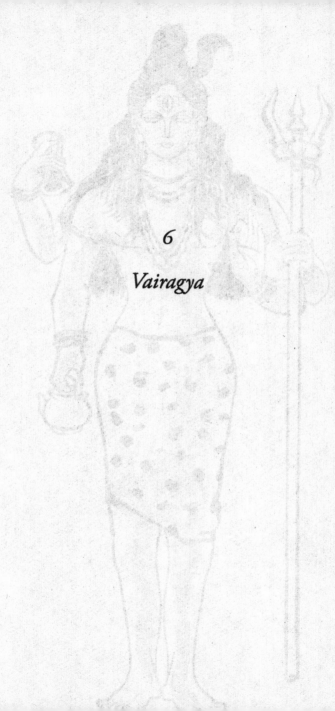

6

Vairagya

Na punyam na papam na saukhyam na duhkham
Na mantro na tirtham na veda na yagyah
Aham bhojanam, naiva bhojyam, na bhokta
Chidanandarupah Shivoham Shivoham.

—'Nirvanashatakam', Shankaracharya[1]

[I am neither virtue nor vice, Neither pleasure nor pain
Neither mantra nor sacred place, Neither Vedas nor
sacrifices
I am neither the food nor the eater, nor the act of eating
I am consciousness and bliss
I am Shiva! I am Shiva!]

Vairagya is detachment, being unruffled in trying
circumstances. The etymology of the Sanskrit term is
vai, which means to become languid, weary or exhausted,[2]

129

and *ragya,* which has to do with emotions. Vairagya, the noun, means change or loss of colour, paleness, disgust, aversion, distaste or loathing. It also means freedom from all worldly desire and indifference to worldly objects and to life—asceticism.[3] That is the specific meaning I am concerned with here. It follows that the one who applies vairagya is a *vairagi.* Much of a vairagi's life is lived inwardly and he endeavours to have neither *raga*—liking—or *dvesha*—dislike. The true vairagi endeavours to control the restless mind through abhyasa or practice.

I risk reinforcing clichés when I mention asceticism as one of the main motifs of Indian culture, but it nevertheless is. First put forward in conjunction with the idea of the mystical Orient, it was believed by many Indologists that Hinduism is only and essentially world-renouncing and ascetic. Though on the surface this may appear to be true, applying a wider lens shows that Hinduism encompasses many other key elements. However, since the ascetic/ renouncer/vairagi tradition has been a kind of leitmotif and often one of the most seminal features of religious life in India, it is crucial to understand its possible meaning for society and its origins. In fact, the ascetic, dedicated to the pursuit of the power of ultimate knowledge, is an important ingredient in the socio-cultural mix that contributed to the very formation of historical religions. This became the core theme of not just Hinduism, but all salvation doctrines, widely advocated in ancient philosophies such as Jainism, Buddhism and Vedanta.

One can gauge the importance of renunciation in the Indian milieu by the different types of renouncers and the several words available for describing them—vairagi, bhikshu, parivrajaka, shramana, sadhu, yogi, rishi, sannyasi and muni, to mention some. These groupings of people share an element of being renunciates but have different doctrines and practices.

Over millennia, many people have found an alternative lifestyle option in renunciation and asceticism. In early Hindu society and even today among orthodox Hindus, individual choice and mobility is, by and large, severely circumscribed by the rigidly stratified caste-based rules. In a way, vairagya provides an 'anti-structure', albeit sanctioned by tradition, providing a meaningful outlet for those who find normal social existence unacceptable.

Shiva is a deity par excellence when it comes to vairagya. His representations in various materials abound with certain specific features: semi-shut eyes, an enigmatic half smile on his lips—as though he is contemplating the long-forgotten truths of the universe through meditation—a straight back, a taut chest, as if concentrating on the rhythmic breathing vital to pranayama, and legs folded in padmasana or sukhasana. In the scriptures, he is the ultimate anchorite, living in forest hermitages, surviving on roots and fruits, cut off from social intercourse. Alternatively, he dwells on Himalayan peaks in Kailash, mostly involved in tapas and meditation, and is now and then called upon by celestial folk to intervene in scuffles with anti-gods. Shiva withdraws from the rest of the world, and many myths abound to illustrate the futility of distracting him from his deep meditation.

At another level he is a householder—a much-loved husband and a much-admired father. In this role, Shiva does not abstain from the pleasures of the body or the bliss of having a family. The contradiction may be resolved by stating that even then he is a vairagi as his asceticism lies in his ability to control and regulate his mind and emotions. This is true of him in all matters of life. Even when he is in a blissful state, he is detached. The road Shiva travels, that lets him be both the ascetic and the householder, shows the kind of lateral thinking where two or more different aspects of a personality can be accommodated. The unease he may encounter—or rather that the believer has to grapple with—is resolved in the myths that try to give a raison d'etre for his seemingly dual life.

When we examine Shiva's trajectory in history, he initially appears to be detached and solitary, living a life of quiet repose. However, he eventually has to save the world by marrying Sati, his first spouse. He gets so attached to her that he completely loses control at her death. He is swallowed by abysmal grief. Oblivious and uncaring, he wallows in his own deep misery, which is so expressive yet so much his own that no one can step in. If the god who is the greatest of the greatest, Mahadeva, can descend into such a state, one can imagine the condition of the world and the lowly souls existing in it. Shiva's incapability to handle this tragic turn in his life causes massive mayhem. Something has to be done to make Shiva a vairagi once again.

We are all aware that mourning for the dead is crucial. Howling, weeping and lamenting can even prove to be cathartic. In fact, even if someone goes through a tragedy stonily, dry-eyed, they eventually have to let the grief manifest. 'Grief' is almost personified as a monster, comfortably making its home inside you, harming you until it is let out. Even after the initial shock, it can lead to dire health issues if one dams the flow of tears and allows sadness to take residence in one's heart.

Yet, mourning should not be endless. Balance has to be restored, and for this the main quality to be invoked is detachment—as the cliché goes, life must go on. But Shiva, oblivious to everything, mourns with no limit. He carries the limp, semi-scorched, dead Sati on his shoulder, moving about the world dancing the Tandava, the dance of grief, with no awareness of time or anything else. A corpse cannot and should not be kept for long. There are all kinds of malodorous consequences, amid other concerns.

Living beings, vibrant and warm, become a mentally and physically harmful presence in no time, once the prana is snuffed out. No, the dead cannot live among the living; the corpse has to be dispensed with. All of Shiva's cronies are incapable, at such a time, to provide solace. They fear him and are themselves mourning, shocked by Sati's sudden death. Sati, whom they had just recently welcomed in their midst, with much fanfare, as the bride of Shiva. A bereft Shiva is helped in such a situation by Vishnu, who is sometimes portrayed as his arch-rival. Vishnu advises Shiva to bid Sati farewell so she can be at peace in her onward journey, and so Shiva can resume his life and get back to his major task as a god. The myth exemplifies how at one level Shiva is detached as a vairagi, yet, when the time comes, he can't get over his grief—therein lies the poignancy of the Shiva–Sati tale. In this state of loss, nothing makes sense to the main representative of this virtue of vairagya. Shiva must learn how to detach all over again. The teacher must relearn a philosophy of which he was the founder, proponent and main adherent. Since everything Shiva is involved in is so intense, it is but natural that his sorrow also has enormous proportions. In fact, it is so extreme that the world stops functioning. Vishnu can see no other way out of this situation except by doing a drastic yet effective dismembering of Sati. Using one of his *ayudha*s, the chakra, he chops off limb after limb, organ after organ, Her body parts fall gently on the earth and become potent spots of her energy. We are told that Shiva takes refuge in her yoni as the linga; in another instance, he moves away once again from the talking, walking, eating, drinking world and takes refuge in silence, a silence that grows beautiful and reinvigorates him.

In what is often called the 'trinity' of the Hindu pantheon, Brahma is the Creator, Vishnu is the Preserver and Shiva is the Destroyer. This formula has been continuing unchallenged over the centuries. But as we study mythology, we find many aspects which contradict this division and characterization. Shiva, according to this prescription, is the Destroyer, but surprisingly, in popular mythology, there are various episodes in which Shiva is approached to save the world from destruction. By his actions, he preserves, saves and stabilizes the world. All these actions are part of his personality and it would indeed be an injustice to associate the mighty deity with only acts of destruction.

Alternatively, one may ask, if he is indeed the Destroyer, is destruction all that bad? For, isn't it only after one destroys the old that the new can take birth? Metaphorically, one can claim that Shiva is a 'destroyer' as he destroys the ego, anger and lust which lie within us and in so many members of the celestial world. He even annihilates the ego within himself and hence emerges as a better 'being'. The presence of ego among his traits gets manifested in his anger and passion, but through meditation, Shiva extinguishes it and emerges new and renewed to face the world and its myriad problems. In the heavenly world, we are told that deities squabble and have ego clashes among themselves. Shiva is rarely part of these shenanigans. He is often implored to take part and show everyone the power of detachment.

Shiva's detachment is an 'attached detachment' for the sake of the world he has to intervene in. He displays his attachment in a totally indifferent manner, as the following myth will amply illustrate. What will also be illustrated is the way the other two main gods behave towards each other, with their inflated egos. Recounted in the Shiva Purana, the myth is a consequence of the first encounter between Brahma and Vishnu.

Vishnu is enjoying slumber on his serpent couch, surrounded by his spouse, Lakshmi, and various attendants. Brahma arrives and asks Vishnu who he is and gets angry with him as even after seeing him Vishnu does not get up, like a haughty person. Brahma claims to be Vishnu's lord, after all. 'An honourable elderly person comes to visit and you behave like such a haughty fool.' Now it is Vishnu's turn to get angry, and he tells Brahma to sit on the couch and not be so agitated, 'for I am the protector of the world and your protector as well'. Vishnu continues, saying, 'The whole universe is situated within me and your way of thinking is like that of a thief. After all, you are born from the lotus sprung from my navel region. You are my son; your words are therefore futile.' Arguing like this and saying each is greater than the other and claiming to be the lord, they get ready to fight like two foolish goats desirous of killing each other.[4] What begins as a casual conversation turns into a bitter quarrel and assumes a catastrophic form.

Seated on their respective vahanas, they examine one weapon after the other, furiously preparing for an awful showdown. Different groups of devas moving about in their aerial chariots come to witness this spectacle. They swiftly realize, once the fight begins, that this is far from entertaining. The world is about to come to an end, *pralaya*, resulting in utter chaos. The sun stops shining, the moon stops appearing, rivers stop flowing and the seasonal cycle of the world goes awry. The devas, in helpless agitation and vexation, talk among themselves. They think of Shiva in their fright and go to his abode in Mount Kailash. They weep tears of joy when they see him and beg him to come and save the world. He always listens when his devotees ask for help, so he accompanies them back to the battleground, so to say. On espying the battle, Shiva vanishes in the firmament and rises in the terrific form of a huge column of fire. Both Brahma and Vishnu are astonished. They cannot see the beginning or end. They have never encountered anything so powerful and enigmatic. Brahma sets out to find the top of the pillar by assuming the form of a gander. Vishnu attempts to get to the bottom as Varaha, his boar avatar. When both of them finally meet after this ordeal of search, Brahma asks Vishnu if he had been able to reach the bottom. Vishnu says he could not find the bottom after trying for many years. Brahma, however, lies and says that he had reached the top.

This is when Shiva appears dramatically from an aperture in the pillar. He punishes Brahma for lying and praises Vishnu for his genuine curiosity and easy admittance to failure and thereby his ability to accept defeat. Vishnu, by being truthful, exemplifies his strength of character and attitude by acknowledging his powerlessness in front of Shiva. He accepts and bows to Shiva's power. This myth tells us that Shiva is the most powerful god and also explains why Brahma had to be punished. Shiva is seen saying, 'O Brahma, in order to extort honour from the people, you assumed the role of the lord in a roguish manner. Hence, you shall not be honoured, nor shall you have your own temple or festival.'[5] Today, the temple in Pushkar, Rajasthan, seems to be the lone temple to Brahma, which in itself is remarkable in this country of temples. The most obvious lesson, of course, is that veracity will triumph and lying will only lead to disastrous consequences. The myth also illustrates why Shiva is supreme and also reveals to us the idea of rivalry which exists between the gods of the Hindu pantheon. The last part of this myth, which speaks of Shiva emerging from an opening of the linga, is often rendered in stone sculpture, mainly from south India. The sculpture type is called Lingavirbhava and Lingodbhava.

Detachment means being calm in any state—in extreme happiness or during the setbacks one faces in a lifetime. On a mundane level, it means finding a way to deal with the growing demands, injustices and burdens that demand our attention in our day-to-day lives, and trying not to get so enmeshed that the vicissitudes of life completely take over. Regardless of the difficulty of the situation, we must not get too agitated. Things often do not work exactly the way we want, for even if we 'fix' our own attitude and responses, we still have to deal with a world filled with other human beings over whom we have little control. All of them may not necessarily be at the same level of emotional maturity as you. Hence, it is best to cultivate a certain level of detachment. It will help us if we understand and assimilate this very important concept and trait as early in life as possible. It applies to both stations in life: extremely disturbing situations and periods of good fortune. The dictum, 'This too shall pass', helps us in all situations.

> *To know*
> *Happiness and sadness*
> *are like friends and foes,*
> *that come and go,*
> *neither will last forever.*

So, we might as well not get too excited by any kind of situation. To borrow from the delightful British idiom: Let's not get our knickers in a twist over something that is bound to change.

Many people mistake detachment for complete abstinence. Vairagya can mean giving up something we love, albeit for a short duration, not perennially. To me, it also means giving up something that is harmful to us. We can extend the idea of vairagya to other parts of our lives. To maintain peace, to expand, to grow, we need to detach ourselves from certain people. All of us inherit relationships that we did not choose—they can be loving, amusing, unbearable or plain toxic. The earlier we realize which ones are not conducive to our well-being, the better.

It is difficult to detach from immediate family whom you, perforce, have to meet now and then, at family gatherings such as weddings, birthdays and festivals. What would be helpful at the outset is to acknowledge what most of us probably know—we give far too much importance to blood relationships. As we know, we can't choose our family. However, we can cease to give it an inordinate amount of importance and not spend a lifetime trying to achieve a semblance of closeness with all members. Sure, one has a superimposed bond of shared parentage but the actual closeness is something people have to work on. It is not a given. So even if we have a sibling who makes us feel awful each time we speak to them, we still soldier on, trying, crying, getting frustrated as they bring out the worst in us, inducing us to yell and behave like a banshee. I have seen perfectly even-keeled, good-tempered, mild-mannered people getting so riled up by a sibling that they become unrecognizable. If it was evident that this behaviour would get them to an easier place to understand each other, I would welcome it. But that doesn't happen, and the same pattern is repeated when they meet again—it is exhausting, self-defeating and futile.

If you can't totally renounce a relationship and cut it off completely, you can choose to make such encounters infrequent. When there are only rare meetings with difficult people, you will be able to withstand the sarcasm or taunts about how neglectful you have been, or even the silent treatment. Better still is to have formal yet cordial relationships. Don't strive for the same closeness that you may have shared earlier, or that you may have with your other siblings or friends. Understand that there can be degrees of closeness—it doesn't have to be all love or all hate. With relatives, apply the concept of vairagya, where nothing they say or do really bothers you. This may sound unnatural to some, but what I mean is try not to let a remark from them derail you. Sure, you can't totally escape—there is a power in words, especially from someone you have known forever—but at least don't allow it the power to unhinge you to such a degree that it stymies you from achieving the life you want. The important aspect of this renouncing is to do it sans guilt, for if you go about renouncing a relationship with a relative and experience misgivings about it, it is futile. This knowledge of when a relationship should be renounced will come from an understanding of yourself.

I have seen many people who don't meet their siblings for years and are none the worse for it. They claim that by not meeting them they can maintain their own mental stability. They have created their own cocoon of close friends with whom they maintain close and satisfactory relationships. This is definitely easier since there is no emotional baggage and hurtful history. It is with these close friends that people who are cut off from their family members can get empathy and understanding—they will hear just your side of the grouse and you can make it seem favourable to yourself in order to protect yourself. If your relationship with someone who is not a family member is causing you distress, abandon it. Go cold turkey. Don't proceed slowly, as that is sometimes akin to a knife slowly being removed from your chest.

The original historical information regarding renunciation may have come from the Upanishads and Buddhist literature. In ancient times, the fame of India's ascetics spread to the Greek and Roman world. When Alexander of Macedonia reached the river Indus in 327 BCE, he was eager to meet India's holy men. Sculptures of ascetics are known from the earliest period of Indian art. In Gandharan reliefs, they frequently appear in scenes illustrating the life of Buddha. The naturalism of these carvings can be seen in the carefully observed emaciated bodies, long, matted hair, bearded faces, bare bodies and simple clothing. Typically, in stone, ascetics bring their hands together in attitudes of reverence; they crouch in huddled postures or lean heavily on their staffs.

In many spiritual paths and in most of Hindu philosophy, a person aims to achieve a mental state in which he abnegates worldly matters and becomes a vigilant observer rather than a participant. This leads to liberation from life itself, as experienced through one's untrained senses, and a flight, as mentioned earlier, from a reality that is seen as illusory. The various characteristics of asceticism, including tapas, meditation and techniques of altering consciousness or withdrawing it to transcend worldly concerns, offer a new vision of the human condition.

The vairagi gives up domesticity—after all, he is supposed to be nomadic, and roams about begging for food in an almost commanding voice. I can recall this from my childhood. Sometimes they take over different localities and visit homes once a week for a handful of grain, pulses or rice. They can be seen on the outskirts of towns, cooking meals on temporary *chulhas* or hearths. In the sphere of symbolism, the vairagi creates a fire within, called tapas. The practice of meditation, yoga, pranayama and fasting can all be categorized under tapas. This is part of the unflagging, unsparing effort that goes into the achievement of higher things, the suffering through infinite pains. Tapas, the heat of renunciation, of voluntary suffering, gives rise to a purifying inner peace and power that burns away the impurities and weaknesses of human existence. Tapas cleanses the mind and purges all memories and prejudices. The ascetic imagines that he is reborn as a purified higher being. Tapas is a creative force that makes one productive; it is through tapas that extension or expansion takes place and concentration of energies is possible. It is like a burning flame produced with the coordination of willpower and efforts, burning all weaknesses and transforming chaos.

In Vedic creation myths, the world came into being when tapas united with another form of heat: kama, that is, desire. In Pauranika and epic literature, tapas includes a number of severe ascetic practices that cause pain, suffering and self-mortification. These practices are widely regarded as having the ability to generate supernatural powers, which can be used in the world and even in the kingdom of heaven. It is often said that such is the power of tapas that the gods try to prevent ascetics from accumulating an excess of it. Constantly, the gods send apsaras to seduce renunciates or to provoke anger, through which all their accumulated power gets annihilated.

The vairagi exemplifies detachment through his attire, mien and behaviour. He has a complete nonchalance towards his appearance. In Brahminical texts, the renouncer is looked upon with some suspicion because of his denial of Vedic ritual. Later, a kind of compromise is affected— not unusual in Hinduism—renunciation is incorporated and given institutionalized status in the third and fourth ashramas. The well-known division of society into the four stages of life or ashramas—student, householder, hermit and renouncer, and sannyasa—was formalized by the time of the texts called the Dharmasutras, circa fourth century BCE. It was made clear that men could take to renunciation after completing the other stages of life. The fourfold ashrama system may have emerged, in the first place, to counter the popularity of renunciation. The message appears to have been: You can assimilate this in your own life, albeit in a way that will render the least harm to existing social dynamics.

There are escape routes for those who don't want to embrace renunciation full-time. Vairagya can also mean a state of mind or an actual giving up of something for a temporary period. There are degrees of vairagya that you can apply in your life. The layperson uses this power of renunciation in what appears to be, in comparison, small ways. We have all sought this 'power' at one time or the other in our lives, maybe even without knowing. We can renounce anything we wish to and for any period of time—it doesn't have to be forever. I would like to start with one kind of renouncing that most of us are familiar with: fasting. Fasting is associated with austerity, and doing without certain pleasures. Even within the gamut of fasting, there is a taxonomy—there are fasts where no salt is consumed, where no sour food or food made from grains is eaten, where no water is taken, where only fruits are eaten. The person fasting is viewed with tolerance, if not a certain reserved reverence. If they are questioned, they will tell you that one of the reasons they fast is because they become the recipient of an inexplicable numinous power. This could be because they are exercising a firm resolve and they have something in their lives that they are in control of, even if it is over a limited period of time. Most importantly, they feel that the sacrifice will endow them with what they desire. Fasting also brings in the idea of 'delayed gratification'— fast with all sincerity and then feast and enjoy life a little more, after this temporary denying of something you love.

Vairagya can be and is practised by people for different reasons. For me, for instance, when a major school exam was around the corner, I renounced my vanity. I would apply copious amounts of oil in my hair and don plain clothes to prepare for a period of renunciation. The goal was to focus on studying rather than gazing at one's self in the mirror or daydreaming. This was my contribution to the idea of vairagya as a teenager. Later, when television was a part of all of our homes, not switching it on was a big sacrifice, when one could not record or watch what one had missed. Today, some people go off social media when they want to concentrate on what they perceive to be a higher goal. Essentially, giving up something is the key ingredient of vairagya adopted today, fine-tuned or tweaked as we choose. A sacrifice is done knowingly, with the expectation of getting something in return.

The principle can also be applied to a relationship that has been working fine for us, but has now become corrosive. The skill to relinquish it will come if you exercise viveka and know when to give up. Relationships can be hard work, and one feels disloyal to abandon an association that has lasted decades because it does not seem right to let go. However, a time comes in our lives when some detritus has to be abandoned. Loyalty is a highly overrated virtue. What use is a friendship if it is wearing you out?

There are poisons that are particularly virulent to the human condition, which we seem to propagate to our own undoing. Among these is resentment. One of the reasons why resentment tumbles over is from the lack of forgiveness. If you cannot forgive then you are definitely not detached; you are holding on to past hurts. This can paralyse your thoughts and feelings and leaves no room for anything else. Everything is filled with dark clouds of anger, a whole life consumed by thoughts of injuries, slights or insults. What a waste. Do we really want to let a person have such a hold on us? In many cases, the resentment we bear is more destructive than the act that caused it, and thereby we end up harming ourselves. Forgiveness is the solution.

There is one more idea that can help in the moving on process: the knowledge that the person you resent has no idea that you are disturbed by their existence. As you ruin your day with negative thoughts, that person is probably having a perfect day.

But forgiving someone is difficult. It is rendered a tad easier if you have made something of yourself in the interim. Otherwise, forget forgiving, you will spend your days lamenting that you are stuck in a miasma and unable to progress in life because of the harm that was done to you. So, it becomes a vicious circle. Hence, we cannot emphasize enough the importance of finding your niche and excelling at it so you become financially and emotionally comfortable. Largesse is at hand only with those who have a richness of spirit. Otherwise, no matter how much you possess materially, if you are not happy with your life, you will not be able to give, forgive or do anything that requires generosity.

Try not to get affected by what others say. If it is particularly harsh, look at their past behaviour; if it happens repeatedly, try to initiate a discussion with that person. If that doesn't help either, let go of this relationship.

The next vairagya is from memories. 'Death' is taking place all the time. For instance, at each stage of life there is a death of the previous stage. In fact, if 'death' is not taking place then this means no growth is taking place. In middle age, it is not charming to act like a teenager. So, bid farewell to different ages, be free of the shadows of the past. Don't be attached to vicious memories or feel victimized by the past. Alternatively, painting the past as a perfect time is also harmful and affects our ability to live happily. I know many who live so much in their past glory that they don't bother to have any glory in the present.

If you do not detach then you will not reach your full potential as you will be stuck in memories of the past. So, don't treat everything in your past as dead, but have the wisdom to know what aspect of your past you can use to your betterment. We all need to have some memories to fall back on in dire times; they can be a lifeline in times of depression. The trick is to know how to separate them from others.

Take the best and use it to your advantage. Cherry-pick memories, staple them and let them be your fix when you are down. Relive that passionate kiss that went on and on despite the pouring rain, despite the annoyed people scuttling by. Recall the fun you had with your siblings, putting up plays and singing competitions, rolling downhill on half-broken cycles, just being together. Relive accolades. Gloat privately over compliments that were unusual and hugely exaggerated. Bring them out, air them, sun them, milk them dry, use them when you need them the most. They are your own and are not harming anyone. I use them as my armour, my 'go to' when I'm down. It is all part of being wise, knowing what to overlook or detach yourself from, and what to use for that boost—needed so often as the frugality of age sets in.

The clutter we have in our homes crowds and overwhelms us and therefore should be periodically gotten rid of. The same maxim applies to the brain—we must learn how to end our relationship with the past and not constantly fret over it. Carrying painful memories makes us less alert and sensitive to the present, for the mind has just so much space. Be alert to the danger of mental overload as the brain can get overtaxed. Teach your mind to exercise a qualitative bond with the past. Instead of ruminating or rehashing over problems, choose to reflect, which is harmless. Several thought patterns that are negative and unhealthy, like cynicism, hostility, anger, jealousy and lack of forgiveness, lead to physical harm and can cause major diseases.

Renounce those happenings in your life that are capable of causing lifelong phobias. Ask the girl who was sexually molested at age seven, first by men known to her father and later by her own uncle and grandfather. Commendably, unlike in many cases, she gathered the courage to tell her parents. Her mother displayed a tired indifference and her father dismissed it. In another case, when Anita was just nine, her mother told her to go and sleep on the common terrace with her uncle and younger sister, due to the lack of space in the house. Even after telling her mother of his attempt to molest her, he was not banished from their midst and she had to live with the memories, as well as the lascivious uncle. When she confronted her mother about that particular incident many decades later, her mother said she was being protective of her other daughter, who was approaching puberty and was also vulnerable to being sexually attacked. The girl grew up to dread sexual relationships and even fostered resentment towards her mother.

A happy childhood with warm parental relationships has long-lasting effects and the power to extend positivity across decades. What about those individuals who had difficult, challenging childhoods? Difficult though it is, stop blaming your parents for everything that has gone wrong in your life. Forgive, if you can. In the close circle of the immediate family or the extended one of cousins and aunts and uncles, certain bonds that at one time looked like nothing could ruin them can get contaminated. For the sake of memories we hold dear and due to a sense of loyalty, we stay with these relationships. If both sides are willing to have a discussion and work out their problems, and also be willing to admit where they were to blame, something can be salvaged. In fact, at times, the relationship might even become more meaningful with the flotsam and jetsam out of the way. However, there will be some people who just want to blame you for everything, and if this is the case then it is not worth bothering about. It is not fair to apportion blame on just one person when a relationship goes sour. The onus of a relationship gone wrong must be shared.

Another renouncing which would be very helpful to us is to relinquish the desire for external approval. You alone are the judge of your worth. You know what your childhood has been about and what you have had to work through to get where you are. Here I would say listen to advice but decide for yourself what you would be able to tolerate and what you want from your life. For instance, I know someone who decided she didn't want to have children and despite others telling her she should, she and her spouse discussed it and they came to a decision. They gave away some of their money to charity and led a life replete with activities they were interested in.

Look at the calm face of Shiva. He does not seem to hanker after anyone's approval. It does not express pain, nor does it betray the suppression of concealed suffering. In most of his manifestations, Shiva takes away all pangs of pain and suffering. I believe that one can strive to eventually be like Shiva and transmit peace and calmness.

Shiva never bothered about what anyone was gossiping about him. He took insults in his stride and stayed close to those who were loyal and loving towards him, like all his ganas and hordes of yoginis. They fought for him and went off on missions for him and accompanied him everywhere.

Every individual has a personal history which is partly responsible for their attitude towards life. It is useful to help justify and understand your behaviour, and then you continue with life. Sometimes, one's personal history is harsh and has a lasting effect whereby it is not just a passive presence in the memory. In such a case, something has to be done about it. I find that it is best to not just dwell on it, but seek professional help. It is akin to a sleeping demon ready to roar when things go downhill due to some extraneous factor, and then boom—it spills all over, messing up your present. So deal with it so that its poisonous reach is mitigated to a non-harmful level.

Another method to tackle one's history or inner clutter—and the method I am addicted to—is writing in a journal. I have been doing it ever since I learnt how to write and was gifted a diary that had a lock and key. It thrilled me to address this faceless 'person' every day as 'Dear Diary'. From fights with siblings to crushes in school, to hating someone or the other you are not actually supposed to hate—everything was poured out, everything was talked through. Today, I continue to write. I love the feel of pen on paper and find that removing the immediate past on to another medium clears my head.

Consciously suspend the ego's tendency to shield itself from the transformative power of introspection. Let's say you do introspect, but only see situations where you have been wronged—such introspection is counterproductive. It is better to see how someone spoke to you as a reflection of what you are. Even if a person is using you as a punching bag, consider whether they are having a bad day themselves.

Introspection can therefore make you feel better about yourself or even make you transform into a calmer person.

Detachment means having a calm exterior and a steady way of being despite the innumerable setbacks one faces in a lifetime. It means finding a way to deal with the overwhelming demands, injustices and burdens that threaten us every day. Regardless of how hard we try to cope the best we can, we must not get agitated when things do not work out exactly the way we want—as human beings we deal with a world filled with other human beings. We can't control all of them and hence must maintain a certain level of detachment. The secret is to learn to maintain it to the right degree.

This principle of detachment is closely linked with resilience and growing a thick skin. We have to keep relearning not to take things personally. People are going to misunderstand us, reject our ideas and attack us, but we have to look at these situations as instigation caused by their personal history rather than a pointer to something lacking in us. Understanding this will keep us protected and enable us to detach instead of getting embroiled in feelings like 'how dare she say that to me?' This is a waste of time and if we still can't shake it off, then we must recognize that we are not here to make everyone happy.

Cultivate vairagya in yourself. When one gets unhinged or derailed and when one runs around like a headless chicken, the best solution seems to be escaping to a quiet destination away from everyone. Since we can't always escape, the best thing to do is to have the quality of vairagya and activate it at such times, like a switch that needs to be turned on within oneself. For we will find that we can't always make the move to different cities or resign from a job or terminate a relationship, but we can change the way we perceive them and have a neutral attitude towards situations. We can become detached and not be so acutely disturbed by what is, at the moment, unchangeable. Another idea that makes detachment easier is if you understand and accept the ephemeral nature of life. Everything has to change in any case—people will go away, seasons will change, you will age. Ultimately, vairagya means to be like a lotus leaf, to originate and live in the murky waters of life without being touched or polluted by it.

Shiva embodies and epitomizes one of the kernels of the Hindu ethos—that life should be 'activistic' and meditative, because life itself comprises both contemplation and action. He can be the ideal of poise and reflection, and this very same meditative action prepares him and gets him ready for action. First the idea takes shape in the mind through deep thinking and then representation takes place via action. Shiva shows that the root of all action is contemplation.

7

Purnatva

Purna madaha
Purna midam
Purnarta purna mudchyute
Purna asya
Purnam adaye purnameva vashishyate
Aum shanti shanti shantihi.

—Shvetashvatara Upanishad[1]

[All this is full
All that is full
From fullness, fullness comes.
When fullness is taken from fullness
Fullness still remains.
Aum shanti shanti shanti]

*P*urna means full, abundant, rich. It refers to a completeness that is experienced within and which practically nothing can affect. Even if terrible circumstances cause depletion in abundance, it still remains. *Purnatva* is the attainment of a condition of ampleness and sufficiency that is not temporary. It is not exactly happiness, but the realization of something more enduring, a feeling of complete and comforting security.

We have discussed the need for focus, detachment, balance and recognizing one's uniqueness and the importance of having someone in your life to love. Equipped with these characteristics, there is a hope that the feeling of purnatva will, in due course, permeate and animate your very being, leading to a sense of wholesomeness. Purnatva is synonymous with the attainment of bliss, your own personally created bliss. It is a consciousness. You will know when you have achieved this state. People around you will sense it. Among other things, it is to experience lucidity of thought, freedom from envy and openness of mind. It is a lofty feeling where there is a consciousness of one's role in this lifetime. It is to feel a sense of integration, an overwhelming feeling and experience of fusion. It is an attitude, to focus on living a life where you are able to give of yourself and yet not feel empty. To be like an overflowing magical *kalash*—even when so much gets removed in everyday life, you have the ability to find pleasure in whatever is left. The residual becomes the essential while the process of gathering and building continues.

So many of us lead lives full of hushed nervousness and claustrophobic anxiety. We hope to be saved—by someone, by a new possession, by a change in surroundings.

This is not always possible or feasible. Importantly, it is not even enough. Time has proved it again and again. We all know and have experienced that life is full of problems—micro and macro—and suffering is a major part of creation. Whether we encounter anguish in small doses or as galactical sorrow, either way, nobody is spared. Everybody experiences setbacks in some phase or in some form or the other. No single person escapes this existential truism. It is truly striking how this universality of suffering gives us so much comfort.

Some people are completely crushed by sad occurrences. Steeped in misery, this becomes their leitmotif, their excuse for everything that goes wrong in an entire lifetime. Then there are those who give you the impression that they have been brought up on a bed of roses and continue to live on it. You might get increasingly annoyed by such people and be convinced that they are experts at acting. You will be wrong, for they are the ones openly in love with life. No, not in a vacuous sort of way where they are to be pitied for being delusional, but by having genuine enthusiasm about life, no matter what it has doled out to them. They get up and dust themselves off after a disaster, work out their issues, seek alternatives for the missing parts of their lives, and soldier on. This is their trademark: the ability to carry on—not just make do—with zest.

They have arrived at a state of purnatva.

Whatever be the case, how we respond to life is an art, a skill. If we are equipped with purnatva, we can help ourselves out of the worst morass, for we will be relying on something we have consciously striven for, something that is eternal and can be rebooted when depleted, something that requires nothing but our own tuned mind as the magic wand. When we are feeling fragmented and things are not working out the way we envisaged, we are hopeful that it is only a brief interlude before the sense of completeness is restored. Purnatva is something that we can manufacture, store and keep with us.

I feel many images of Shiva show this aura of purnatva. One of his forms, Dakshinamurti, holds a special place. In this form, Shiva is the guru, imparting the knowledge of yoga, the shastras and music, among other things. Most importantly, he is teaching ultimate knowledge, that is, supreme awareness. In this iconographic form, Shiva is shown with a blissful expression under a banyan tree, surrounded by sages. He is seated with one leg on his thigh and the other touching the ground. His fingers are positioned in the hand gesture called *chinamudra*, which is identified by the tip of the thumb touching the index finger. He is smiling and silent, teaching through meditation. A second interpretation of this form touches upon the meaning of *dakshina*, which means south in Sanskrit—the belief is that the south represents the direction of death. Shiva stands for the death of all kinds of things; not just physical death but the death of ignorance, thereby bringing about fruitful change and transformation through self-knowledge. The sages had entreated the lord to remove *avidya*, a kind of spiritual ignorance, and teach them how to attain salvation.

Purnatva can be seen in those who have freedom from craving and desire. For instance, if you are content with your own home and material possessions even as the homes of your friends, colleagues or siblings get grander and grander, you have attained purnatva. It does not mean that you have relinquished the joy of earning money and having beautiful objects, but that once you have got what you dreamt of, you have no greed for more—this feeling will make you experience a rarely encountered contentment. Nothing is more unattractive than a person who constantly complains and is bursting with insatiable desire and greed. Nothing is more attractive than a person who is satisfied with how their life is proceeding.

One of Shiva's epithets is Ashutosh, which means easily satisfied. This refers to how undemanding he is of his followers and worshippers in terms of what they offer him in rituals—flowers, fruits and water are poured on the linga, his aniconic form, with which he is most popularly worshipped. A number of myths convey that he is practically indifferent to what is offered to him and is more concerned with the feelings that accompany his worship.

Some self-help books say things like 'Don't work for money, but for love'—this is rubbish! The person with purnatva works, earns money and is financially independent. He has a sensible relationship with money and recognizes that one needs to have a certain amount of it all the time in order to be sanguine. You cannot possibly be peaceful if you have to wonder where your next meal will come from. Without enough money, we forsake another passage to joy—the ability to help someone, or just give someone a treat or a gift. Sure, many acts of kindness can be done sans recourse to cash, but a large number are facilitated with the help of money. Another issue is that if you fall gravely ill, who will bear the expenses?

I can cite many examples to illustrate that the presence or abundance of money doesn't automatically mean a hedonistic, self-centred life. It is hypocritical to denounce it and need it all the same. Money is extremely crucial if you live to be old, with all the ailments and demands that accompany old age. It is awful if you have to ask your offspring or others for financial help. Purnatva entails having a steady source of income.

The purnatva person is curious about others. This is crucial because a lack of curiosity will end up making you seem smug and—as a natural concomitant—friendless, for who likes to be around a person who has no interests? If you are so self-sufficient that you don't need to know about anyone else, it reflects a vanity that can make you very boring. It can also give rise to an attitude of megalomania and deprive you from learning as you keep yourself distanced from other people's life experiences.

Another trait that we should try to cultivate is compassion. Understanding others and their lives, pains and shortcomings will go a long way in making us empathetic. Purnatva means we have compassion; it means we live without guilt and regret. When someone needs us, especially the elderly, we should not only tend to them but make them feel like they are all that concerns us. Whether in person or through another medium like the telephone, we should listen with hundred per cent attentiveness and genuinely not seem bothered about receiving any gratitude in return. This is how we will never have a sense of guilt or the 'what if' feeling that gnaws away from the inside and does so much damage. I know of at least four elderly people who have told their relatives, 'Don't wait for me to die to show me how much I have meant to you. Do it now while I am living.' The purnatva individual does not need to be told any such thing. So, don't have any regret where the seniors in your life are concerned; do for them as much as you can and live without guilt.

Pour everything you can into every role you play in life. Even as a mother, for instance, your experience of motherhood will change as your child grows from infancy to adolescence and then adulthood. That is precisely why we should keep examining our lives to see what our priorities are at each stage. The roles we play should be in sync with the most important demand at that particular phase.

Purnatva in a person can be recognized when they get happiness from what appears to be the smallest of reasons:

when they encounter no traffic signals on the road, when a favourite song plays on the radio or when they get a place to sit on the bus. Even such simple things are enough to trigger a buoyant state of mind in them. We can also see purnatva when a person praises a colleague heartily with no hidden agenda or envy, letting the world know how accomplished he or she is.

A person endowed with purnatva is a keen observer. They will experience a heightened awareness; they may begin to hear ambient sounds they had never heard before, like the chirping of an uncommon bird. They will be intuitive and pick up on others' sad thoughts and be ready to help, if needed. If you have arrived at purnatva, you will feel *ananda*, the consciousness of bliss. You will experience the 'oceanic feeling'. You will begin to act out of your higher nature. As a natural corollary to this, people around you will start treating you well, and all your tasks will get done effortlessly.

People who have achieved purnatva pick up skills throughout their lives. They live in an organized manner and hence have the time and energy to learn new things, regardless of their age. These skills could be anything: driving, cooking, knitting, dancing or learning a new language.

I know a man who has been a successful surgeon. He seemed to have nearly everything one could desire: a huge seaside mansion equipped with a jacuzzi, a swimming pool, artwork from all over the world, and a yacht. He had loving relationships with his immediate and extended family. Then, in his fifties, he decided to do something absolutely new—he took up cooking. He wanted to be creative and include all the people he loved in this new-found hobby. It was a joy watching him download recipes, scour farmers' markets for rare ingredients and make personalized menus for guests. We saw a totally different side of him when we visited and he looked like he was brimming over with purnatva, full of humour, generosity, modesty, and with time for everyone. He didn't take up this hobby due to necessity or as a way out of boredom—just for the sheer joy of learning something new, and connecting with and pleasing those he loved most. He claimed he couldn't ask for more from life, and to hear someone say that is truly a wonder.

People who are in a state of purnatva don't cling to their children, siblings or spouse all the time. They seem to have their own little getaways. They set out to teach someone how to read, use a computer or play scrabble, or they tell a lonely person a story and encourage them to share the stories of their childhood. Basically, they give you their time. They know how to make themselves matter. They never feel redundant.

Start young. Have an inner alertness. One of the biggest challenges we have to counter is the tendency to be drifters. Don't drift. Take action as soon as you can, for all inner changes take time. You think it takes long to get slim thighs or a flat tummy? You have no idea how much time inner streamlining takes. It is easier to see which part needs to be worked on if one is overweight, but internal flaccidness is rarely apparent. That's where meditation comes in. The first step is to feel enthused enough to attempt it. What if you have a blasé mindset or are too cynical? That's another hurdle you will have to overcome. You can achieve this by doing something you find meaningful, something that will bring out the best in you.

So do something which makes you connect to your childhood fancies, something you can take pride in, something you have a proclivity towards, and make it a part of your life. For instance, if singing is your passion but you don't have the means to train for it, go sing with gusto in temples or churches, or join a choir or a group that sings bhajans together. Take the initiative.

Purnatva can also be accessed by reliving a happy memory, humming a favourite song, finishing that article or project, basking and accepting praise with joy—we can increase the intensity and duration of positive experiences and emotions when we recall them at a later date.

So savour these moments. We are able to recall a particular memory so vividly because we luxuriated in the experience while deeply engaging with it. A useful 'tool' is to learn to rewind and relive a glorious time in your life again and again.

When you savour an experience, you deliberately enhance and prolong a positive mood, experience and emotion. You can do this by pausing, closing your eyes and appreciating a moving musical performance, for instance. Similarly, when you are feeling sad or hopeless, try to make sure you remember every aspect of happier times.

Savour not just good food but a conversation, a piece of fine writing, anything that is joyful.

To remain content is an art. When you embrace purnatva, you will realize that the cause for contentment is wisdom. You are discerning in whatever you do. Wisdom means emancipation not only from ignorance but from anguish and suffering. Gyana is knowledge and viveka is wisdom. The constant pursuit of knowledge is necessary as a daily activity; it helps us keep pace with changes in technology and in the world in general. Knowledge is easily locatable—so much of knowledge is facts and figures. But you have to search for wisdom wherever you can.

Take help. Read. Books are an alternative pleasurable education about life. They can be books that prepare you for the existential crisis you will inevitably face at some stage, or candid memoirs that will take you into the lives of people who admit where they went wrong. Some self-help books are delightful too. Even the number of online courses or books and seminars on personal development has increased exponentially. Watch sensitively made movies or television that can give you insights into your own situation. Try and lead the best life you can and flourish. You can't steal it from anybody; you have to experience it and then want it to become your way of being.

Having said this, purnatva does not mean a life of aloneness or aloofness. One has to be cautious and guard against a feeling of superiority, or the whole purpose will be defeated. The inner self has to be in constant sync with the outside world. Gravitate towards two types of people: those who inspire, challenge and help you to stay motivated and grounded, and those with whom you share a camaraderie, like friends and relatives. Not those people with whom you share just your accolades, but those with whom you can be honest.

I don't really believe in the maxim, 'A friend in need is a friend indeed'. For, I have experienced that many friends will gather around you when you are 'in need' in an almost voyeuristic manner, to see your sorrow. Then they will lap up all the praise bestowed on them by onlookers for being so thoughtful. Some will feel much better about themselves when they see how miserable you are, and will silently pat themselves on the back by thinking their own marriages are stronger or their offspring relatively more well-behaved. But how many of us can claim to have friends when we are flourishing? How many of our friends will enjoy our achievements? Fortunate is the person who has acquaintances who will bask in their reflected glory.

Friendships are dicey. If you do much better than your friends, they might feel insecure or jealous. Often, the reason some people have many friends is not just because they are likeable—much more goes into this then you can imagine. But, whatever the case, you have to have friends, even if it is just three or four. Try to have more than a couple. Go to them for different needs and the different kinds of times you want to enjoy in their company. One could be the cerebral friend with whom you exchange books and have lengthy discussions on a wonderful turn of phrase or the plot of a novel. You could have one with whom you like drinking and reminiscing. Another friend could be the one you like to gossip with about your common workplace, and another could be the person with whom you discuss family matters. Never have just one—do not put all your eggs in one basket as friendships are difficult to sustain. To keep up friendships, a crucial element is having the ability to show vulnerability. That always increases closeness.. Secondly, we should have the energy of compassion within us. If we have this one trait, we will be able to relate to our friends and to the world at large, and thereby get out of the prison of our loneliness. Those who have no compassion are lonely because they have no way and no desire to understand others. They judge people all the time. They won't accept that people are different and are dealing with different circumstances in their lives.

People with purnatva engage with you. They don't believe that they know it all, and are searching for meaning by chatting, by enquiring, by observing, by getting to know you. We must stay clear of cynicism. Many of us stop being enamoured about new experiences as we assume responsibilities and build routines. We become blasé and get that look of 'been there, done that'. Our sense of wonder starts to escape us. We are born curious but our insatiable drive to learn, explore and study takes us far away from others' lives.

Genuine improvement makes us clear-thinking people comfortable in our own skin. Sometimes we meet people who have an aura of calm, compassion and chutzpah. No, they are not necessarily saintly. They have savoir faire. Everything they do has finesse, elan. We can be greatly moved by interacting with such people. Their suaveness does not come from material possessions or luxury, but a poise derived from self-examination, from experiencing the self deeply. They seem to have a high degree of emotional awareness. Such a presence is very compelling and affords a view of the vast horizons that are open to us due to the slow erosion of ignorance, self-absorption, lassitude and pessimism.

They say that Shiva is within us, but his inscrutable and beautiful outer form provides as much solace. Look at Shiva as depicted in the plastic arts. Whether standing tall or seated, he has the aura of purnatva—a reassurance, a confidence drawn from his own unique qualities. Whether he is deciding what course of action to take, whether he is making love or bantering with his beloved, everything springs from a deep reservoir of well-being.

Expect the unexpected from Shiva, and, by extension, from life. In unique ways, he also calls attention to the marginalized—such as the dwarfed, hunchbacked or strange-looking and oddly behaving ganas he chose to pass his time with. It is not surprising, then, that brigands, robbers, drunkards and other sections of society that live in the margins all identify with Shiva. Everyone is the same for Shiva, regardless of whether they are considered impure or not—all restrictions are man-made and do not matter.

A successful person is one who is not routinely agitated and has a great amount of equanimity. All kinds of austerities and penance pale in front of the ability to live with equanimity. The serenity of the mind is a thing we must covet, for even if we retire to a mountain or beautiful seashore—environs that are traditionally associated with spirituality—some kind of agitation is always carried in our hearts. We must fine-tune our own souls so we can be peaceful anywhere.

We should aspire to always stay in control of our senses. Besides, keeping our cool helps us retain and conserve energy, which we can use for something positive and productive. When we are at peace with ourselves, everything happening around us can be dealt with more effectively. However, if we have a restless mind, we will have turbulent thoughts which will not only hinder our progress in the material world but also spiritually and in our personal relationships.

Finally, there is no need to strive for salvation if you are living with lavish feelings of generosity, contentment and compassion, because these are all signs of salvation. Those who experience purnatva are not concerned with what they will find after this life or with questions such as whether it will be eternal or not. For them, life is eternal now, and they luxuriate in this knowledge. But if your days are rife with a sense of incompleteness, envy, fear and anxiety and you are unable to find lasting happiness, then the constant desire to attain salvation from this miserable life is but natural.

Experience your resplendence. This will be possible if you maintain equanimity, no matter what the situation. The Indic religion has mastered and provided some laws that govern inner well-being. Indian philosophy places greater emphasis on being content and calm rather than just being happy. It's striking to notice that in the Upanishads, every prayer ends with 'Aum shanti, shanti, shanti'. 'Aum' stands for 'sound of the infinite', while 'shanti' means peace and serenity. Peace is the most valuable thing, the feeling that everybody is striving for. Peace is the motive, the motto and the goal. Historically, the Upanishads became conscious for the first time of the necessity of self-realization, which alone leads to complete liberation from misery.

The main objectives of life are to remove three kinds of obstacles or suffering. This is the reason why 'shanti' is said three times after important prayers. Called *trivaram satyam*, it is said that that which is uttered thrice comes true. The thrice-uttered 'shanti' is not just for peace but to ward off obstructions from three sources.

The first 'shanti' is for *adhidaivika*, that is, the unseen power of divine origin. These are obstacles over which we have no control, such as earthquakes, floods and volcanic eruptions. This 'shanti' is to be chanted loud. The second 'shanti' is chanted for *adhibhautika*, a word derived from *bhuta*, which originates in physical, material beings and from sources over which one has no immediate control. This includes the people around us who can cause problems, accidents and crimes. The third 'shanti' is for oneself: *adhyatmika*. These are obstructions centred on one's own body, the senses and the mind. They are self-inflicted, long-lasting, and include physical, mental and emotional suffering, such as anger, jealousy, hatred and greed. These are the most damaging aspects and are part of our daily lives. This 'shanti' is to be chanted very softly, just for ourselves.

That we all be adequately blessed, Aum shanti, shanti, shanti.

For the reader
for a mind without envy,
without loneliness,
without lassitude,
without agitation.

For a life
with riches
with plenty of work
with caring company
with good health
with compassion.
And the purnatva
that makes it all worth it.

Notes

Chapter 3: Svabhava

1. Swami Tapasyananda, tr., *Sivananda Lahari of Sri Sankaracarya* (Madras: Sri Ramakrishna Math, 1985), p. 77.

2. Devdutt Pattanaik, *7 Secrets of Shiva* (New Delhi: Westland, 2011), p. 37.

3. Sukumari Bhattacharji, *The Indian Theogony* (Delhi: Motilal Banarsidass, 1970), p. 200.

4. J.L. Shastri, ed., *Linga Purana, Part 1: Ancient Indian Tradition and Mythology* (Delhi: Motilal Banarsidass, 1990), pp. 115–16.

Chapter 4: Samarasa

1. Nataraja Guru, tr., *Saundaryalahari of Sankaracarya* (New Delhi: D.K. Printworld, 2008).
2. Chapter 14, Verse 56, *Siva Purana, Part 1: Ancient Indian Tradition and Mythology* (Delhi: Motilal Banarsidass, 1986), p. 336.
3. Ibid, Verse 57.
4. Ibid, Chapter 15, Verse 9, p. 337.
5. Ibid, Verses 25–35, pp. 344–45.
6. Ibid, Verses 55–64, p. 378.
7. Ibid, Verses 66–70.
8. Ibid, Chapter 23, Verses 1–9, p. 379.
9. Ibid, Verses 13–15.
10. Ibid, Verse 39.
11. Ibid, Chapter 26, Verses 10–16.
12. G.P. Bhatt, ed., *Skanda Purana, Vol. 49: Ancient Indian Tradition and Mythology* (Delhi: Motilal Banarsidass, 1992), Chapter 3, Verses 15–23.
13. N.A. Deshpande, tr., *Padma Purana: Ancient Indian Tradition and Mythology, Vol. 2* (Delhi: Motilal Banarsidass, 1990), Chapter 44, Verses 1–2.
14. Ibid, Verses 18–19.
15. Ibid.

Chapter 6: Vairagya

1. Swami Muktananda, *The Nectar of Chanting* (New York: SYDA Foundation, 1984).

2. Sir M. Monier Williams, *A Sanskrit-English Dictionary* (Delhi: Oxford University Press, 2000), p. 1019.
3. Ibid, p. 1025.
4. Chapter 6, Verses 1–9, *Siva Purana, Part 1: Ancient Indian Tradition and Mythology* (Delhi: Motilal Banarsidass, 1986), pp. 52–53.
5. Ibid, Chapter 8, Verses 9–11, p. 58.

Chapter 7: Purnatva

1. Eknath Easwaran, *The Upanishads* (California: Blue Mountain Centre of Meditation, 2007), p. 158.

Bibliography

Primary Sources

Bhatt, G.P., ed. *Skanda Purana, Part 1: Ancient Indian Tradition and Mythology*. Delhi: Motilal Banarsidass, 1992.

Deshpande, N.A., tr. *Padma Purana: Ancient Indian Tradition and Mythology*. Delhi: Motilal Banarsidass, 1990.

Nandargikar, Gopal Raghunath, tr. *The Raghuvamsa of Kalidasa: With the Commentary of Mallinatha*, 1982.

Shastri, J.L., ed. *Linga Purana, Part 1: Ancient Indian Tradition and Mythology*, vols 5–6. Delhi: Motilal Banarsidass, 1990.

Shastri, J.L., ed. *Siva Purana, Part 1: Ancient Indian Tradition and Mythology*. Delhi: Motilal Banarsidass, 1986.

Swami Gambhirananda, tr. *Svetasvatara Upanisad, with the Commentary of Sankaracarya*. Calcutta: Advaita Ashrama, 1995.

Swami Tapasyananda. *Sivananda Lahari of Sri Sankaracarya*. Madras: Ramakrishna Math, 1985.

Tagare, G.V., tr. *Vayu Purana, Part 1: Ancient Indian Tradition and Mythology*, vol. 37. Delhi: Motilal Banarsidass, 1987.

Secondary Sources

Bailly, Constantina Rhodes. *Shaiva Devotional Songs of Kashmir: A Translation and Study of Utpaladeva's Shivastotravali*. Albany: State University of New York Press, 1987.

Bhattacharji, Sukumari. *The Indian Theogony*. Delhi: Motilal Banarsidass, 1970.

Bhattacharyya, N.N. *Indian Demonology: The Inverted Pantheon*. Delhi: Manohar, 2000.

Biardeau, Madeleine. *Hinduism: The Anthropology of a Civilization*, translated by Richard Nice. Delhi: Oxford University Press, 1989.

Cashford, Jules. *The Moon, Myth and Image*. Cassell, 2003.

Chitgopekar, Nilima. *Encountering Sivaism: The Deity, the Milieu, the Entourage*. Delhi: Munshiram Manoharlal, 1998.

Chitgopekar, Nilima. *Rudra: The Idea of Shiva.* New Delhi: Penguin Books, 2007.

Choudhuri, Usha, and Indra Nath Choudhuri. *Hinduism: A Way of Life and a Mode of Thought.* New Delhi: Niyogi Books, 2012.

Clooney, Francis X.S.J. *Hindu Wisdom for All God's Children.* New York: Orbis Books, 1998.

Clothey, Fred W., and J. Bruce Long, eds. *Experiencing Siva: Encounters with a Hindu Deity.* New Delhi: Manohar, 1983.

Das, Gurcharan. *The Difficulty of Being Good.* New Delhi: Penguin Books, 2012.

Davis, Richard H. *Worshiping Siva in Medieval India: Ritual in an Oscillating Universe.* Princeton, NJ: Princeton University Press, 1991.

Dehejia, Vidya, ed. *Devi, the Great Goddess: Female Divinity in South Asian Art.* Washington, DC: Arthur M. Sackler Gallery, 1999.

Dobelli, Rolf. *The Art of the Good Life.* UK: Hodder and Stoughton, 2017.

Easwaran, Eknath. *The Upanishads.* Blue Mountain Centre of Meditation, 2007 (reprint).

Eck, Diana. *Encountering God: A Spiritual Journey from Bozeman to Banaras.* Boston: Beacon Press, 1993.

Eliade, Mircea. *Patanjali and Yoga.* Schocken Books, 1975.

Garcia, Hector, and Francesc Miralles. *Ikigai: The Japanese Secret to a Long and Happy Life*. London: Hutchinson, 2016.

Goldberg, Ellen. *The Lord Who Is Half Woman: Ardhanarisvara in Indian and Feminist Perspective*. Albany: State University of New York Press, 2002.

Gonda, Jan. *Visnuism and Sivaism: A Comparison*. London: Athlone, 1970.

Hiltebeitel, Alf, ed. *Criminal Gods and Demon Devotees: Essays on the Guardians of Popular Hinduism*. Albany: State University of New York Press, 1989.

Iyengar, B.K.S. *Light on the Yoga Sutras of Patanjali*. Noida: HarperCollins, 2008.

Iyer, Pico. *The Art of Stillness: Adventures in Going Nowhere*. New York: Simon and Schuster, 2014.

Kakar, Sudhir. *Culture and Psyche: Selected Essays*. Delhi: Oxford University Press, 1997.

Khandelwal, Meena, Sondra L. Hausner, Ann D. Grodzins Gold, eds. *Nuns, Yoginis, Saints and Singers: Women Renunciation in South Asia*. New Delhi: Zubaan, 2007.

Kramrisch, Stella. *The Presence of Siva*. Princeton, NJ: Princeton University Press, 1981.

Lavin, Edward J.S.J. *Life Meditations*. New York: Wings Books, 1993.

Lorenzen, David. *The Kapalikas and Kalamukhas: Two Lost Saivite Sects*. Berkeley: University of California, 1972.

O'Flaherty, Wendy Doniger. *Asceticism and Eroticism in the Mythology of Siva*. New York: Oxford University Press, 1973.

Pandit, M.P. *Japa*. Pondicherry: Dipti Publishers, 1959, 1977 (reprint).

Pattanaik, Devdutt. *7 Secrets of Shiva*. Chennai: Westland, 2011.

Peck, M. Scott. *The Road Less Travelled*. London: Arrow, 1978.

Peterson, Indira Viswanathan. *Poems to Siva: The Hymns of the Tamil Saints*. Princeton, NJ: Princeton University Press, 1989.

Sharma, Arvind. *Classical Hindu Thought: An Introduction*. Delhi: Oxford University Press, 2000.

Shulman, David Dean. *Tamil Temple Myths: Sacrifice and Divine Marriage in the South Indian Saiva Tradition*. Princeton, NJ: Princeton University Press, 1980.

Sutherland, Stewart, ed. *The World's Religions*. Routledge, 1985.

White, David Gordon. *The Alchemical Body: Siddha Traditions in Medieval India*. Chicago: University of Chicago, 1996.

Zimmer, Heinrich. *Myths and Symbols in Indian Art and Civilization*. Bollingen Foundation, 1946.

ALSO BY NILIMA CHITGOPEKAR

Rudra: The Idea of Shiva

Once feared as the capricious and terrifying Rudra, Shiva, the most 'un-Brahmanic' of gods, has traditionally been shunned by orthodox Vedic religion. Although the Shiva we recognize today retains much of his original contrarian nature, he is firmly ensconced in popular imagination as the awe-inspiring Mahadeva, supreme lord of the universe. In a unique attempt to explore the varied planes of thought and belief that Shiva has represented over millennia, Nilima Chitgopekar imaginatively recreates the defining moments of the great god's life through the eyes of his most intimate mythological companions. Vishnu, Sati, Daksha, Parvati and Ganesha take turns to praise, criticize, explain, complain, sermonize and rationalize—and through the prism of what they choose to reveal of the Shiva they know, there emerges the vision of a god who assimilates in his person the most extreme contradictions. For Shiva is as reclusive as he is accessible, as loved as he is feared, and as fallible as he is divine.

As the author traces the diverse threads of history, philosophy, anthropology and faith that have coalesced to create this intriguing deity, she uncovers the deeper truth about Shiva's unmatched appeal—a credo of simple devotion to a unified godhead, one that reflects the eclecticism and humanity that form the very core of Hindu thought.